Industrial Innovation and International Trading Performance

CONTEMPORARY STUDIES IN ECONOMIC AND FINANCIAL ANALYSIS VOL. 15

Editors: Professor Edward I. Altman and Ingo Walter, Associate Dean
Graduate School of Business Administration, New York University

CONTEMPORARY STUDIES IN ECONOMIC AND FINANCIAL ANALYSIS

An International Series of Monographs

Series Editors: Edward I. Altman and Ingo Walter
Graduate School of Business Administration, New York University

Volume 1. DYNAMICS OF FORECASTING FINANCIAL CYCLES: Theory, Technique and Implementation
Lacy H. Hunt, II, *Fidelcor Inc. and the Fidelity Bank*

Volume 2. COMPOSITE RESERVE ASSETS IN THE INTERNATIONAL MONETARY SYSTEM
Jacob S. Dreyer, *Graduate School of Arts and Sciences, New York University*

Volume 3. APPLICATION OF CLASSIFICATION TECHNIQUES IN BUSINESS, BANKING AND FINANCE
Edward I. Altman, *Graduate School of Business Administration, New York University,* Robert B. Avery, *Graduate School of Industrial Administration, Carnegie-Mellon University,* Robert A. Eisenbeis, *Federal Deposit Insurance Corporation,* and Joseph F. Sinkey, Jr., *College of Business Administration, University of Georgia*

Volume 4. PROBLEM AND FAILED INSTITUTIONS IN THE COMMERCIAL BANKING INDUSTRY
Joseph F. Sinkey, Jr., *College of Business Administration, University of Georgia*

Volume 5. A NEW LOOK AT PORTFOLIO MANAGEMENT
David M. Ahlers, *Graduate School of Business and Public Administration, Cornell University*

Volume 6. MULTINATIONAL ELECTRONIC COMPANIES AND NATIONAL ECONOMIC POLICIES
Edmond Sciberras, *Science Policy Research Unit, University of Sussex*

Volume 7. VENEZUELAN ECONOMIC DEVELOPMENT: A Politico-Economic Analysis
Loring Allen, *University of Missouri, St. Louis*

Volume 8. ENVIRONMENT, PLANNING AND THE MULTINATIONAL CORPORATION
Thomas N. Gladwin, *Centre d'Etudes Industrielles and New York University*

Volume 9. FOREIGN DIRECT INVESTMENT, INDUSTRIALIZATION AND SOCIAL CHANGE
Stephen J. Kobrin, *Sloan School of Management, Massachusetts Institute of Technology*

Volume 10. IMPLICATIONS OF REGULATION ON BANK EXPANSION: A Simulation Analysis
George S. Oldfield, Jr., *Graduate School of Business and Public Administration, Cornell University*

Volume 11. IMPORT SUBSTITUTION, TRADE AND DEVELOPMENT
Jaleel Ahmad, *Concordia University, Sir George Williams Campus*

Volume 12. CORPORATE GROWTH AND COMMON STOCK RISK
David R. Fewings, *McGill University*

Volume 13. CAPITAL MARKET EQUILIBRIUM AND CORPORATE FINANCIAL DECISIONS
Richard C. Stapleton, *Manchester Business School and New York University,* and M. G. Subrahmanyam, *Indian Institute of Management and New York University*

Volume 14. IMPENDING CHANGES FOR SECURITIES MARKETS: What Role for the Exchanges?
Ernest Bloch and Robert A. Schwartz, *Graduate School of Business Administration, New York University*

Volume 15. INDUSTRIAL INNOVATION AND INTERNATIONAL TRADING PERFORMANCE
William B. Walker, *Science Policy Research Unit, University of Sussex*

Volume 16. FINANCIAL POLICY, INFLATION AND ECONOMIC DEVELOPMENT: The Mexican Experience
John K. Thompson, *Mellon Bank, N.A.*

Volume 17. THE MANAGEMENT OF CORPORATE LIQUIDITY
Michel Levasseur, *Centre d'Enseignement Superieur des Affaires, Jouy-en-Josas, France*

Volume 18. STABILIZATION OF INTERNATIONAL COMMODITY MARKETS
Paul Hallwood, *University of Aberdeen*

Volume 19. PROBLEMS IN EUROPEAN CORPORATE FINANCE: Text and Cases
Michel Schlosser, *Centre d'Enseignement Superieur des Affaires, Jouy-en-Josas, France*

Volume 20. THE MULTINATIONAL ENTERPRISE: International Investment and Host-Country Impacts
Thomas G. Parry, *School of Economics, University of New South Wales*

Volume 21. POLICY RESPONSES TO RESOURCE DEPLETION: The Case of Mercury
Nigel Roxburgh, *Management Studies Division, The Economist Intelligence Unit Limited*

Volume 22. THE INTERNATIONAL MONEY MARKET: An Assessment of Forecasting Techniques and Market Efficiency
Richard M. Levich, *Graduate School of Business Administration, New York University*

Volume 23. TRANSNATIONAL CONGLOMERATES AND THE ECONOMICS OF DEPENDENT DEVELOPMENT: A Case Study of the International Electrical Oligopoly and Brazil's Electrical Industry
Richard Newfarmer, *University of Notre Dame*

Volume 24. THE POLITICAL ECONOMY OF ENVIRONMENTAL PROTECTION
Horst Siebert, *University of Mannheim,* and Ariane Berthoin Antal, *International Institute for Environment and Society, Berlin*

Industrial Innovation and International Trading Performance

by WILLIAM B. WALKER
Science Policy Research Unit
University of Sussex

JAI PRESS INC.
Greenwich, Connecticut

Library of Congress Cataloging in Publication Data

Walker, William B
Industrial innovation and international trading performance.

(Contemporary studies in economic and financial analysis; v. 15)
Bibliography: p.
Includes index.
1. Commerce. 2. Technological innovations.
3. Product life cycle. I. Title. II. Series.
HF1007.W25 658.8 77-7777
ISBN 0-89232-083-4

165 West Putnam Avenue
Greenwich, Connecticut 06830

ISBN NUMBER: 0-89232-083-4
Library of Congress Catalog Card Number: 77-7777
Manufactured in the United States of America

CONTENTS

Figures and Tables *xi*
Preface *xiii*

I Theories of International Trade **1**
Ricardian and Heckscher-Ohlin Trade Models 1
Testing the Neoclassical Trade Model 4
The Leontief Paradox 5
Labor skills
Factor-intensity reversals
Resource endowments
Consumer preferences
Technology gap and product cycle
Redefining "capital" and "labor"
Other Theories of International Trade 8
Scale economies
Income levels and consumer preferences
Which Theory? 10

II Technology Gap and Product Cycle Theories **13**
Technology-Gap Model 13
Product-Cycle Theory 14

Validity of Neo-Technology Theories 17

The technology gap theory: tests

The product cycle theory: tests

Product-Cycle "Non-conformists": Textile Machinery 20

Product-Cycle "Conformists": Chemicals 29

Product-Cycle "Conformists": Consumer Electronics 32

Concluding Comments on the Neo-Technology Theories 34

III International Trading Patterns 41

The Growth of World Trade 41

Geographical Concentration of Trade 43

Product Concentration of Trade 47

Product Specialization within the OECD 51

"R&D-Intensity" of OECD Trade 54

IV Innovation and Trading Performance: Statistical Tests 63

Preamble 63

Results of Statistical Tests 67

Foreign investment, licensing and trade

Industries with expected correlation coefficients

Industries with unexpected correlation coefficients

Influence of economic performance on innovative effort

V Final Comments 80

Appendix A

The Measurement of Industrial Innovation **83**

R&D as a measure of innovative activity

Innovative output as a "function" of R&D inputs

Qualitative aspects of innovation

R&D Statistics 89

Product-field vs. industry-group classification

Differences in coverage of R&D surveys from country to country

Problems of disaggregation

Source of funds

R&D-intensities

Consistency of R&D surveys

Appendix B **103**
The Measurement of Trading Performance 103

References 115

Index 119

FIGURES AND TABLES

Figure 1 Characteristics of the product cycle 15
Figure 2 Productivity developments in principle cotton industry processes, 1900–1965. 21
Figure 3 Shearer-Loader development 1954–1973: major machines introduced by machinery manufacturers. 26
Table 1 Foreign trade as a percentage of GDP. 42
Table 2 Industrial production and export trends. 43
Table 3 Intra-OECD exports and imports as a proportion of total OECD trade (1962–1972) 44
Table 4 Shares in intra-OECD trade, 1972. 45
Table 5 USA: destination of exports, 1963–1972. 45
Table 6 EEC: destination of exports, 1963–1972. 46
Table 7 EFTA: destination of exports, 1963–1972. 46
Table 8 Shares of manufactured export trade of ten major OECD countries 46
Table 9 Intra-OECD exports by main SITC product-groups 1962–1972 48
Table 10 OECD intra-trade as a percentage of total OECD trade in SITC product-groups 49
Table 11 U.K.: structure of trade flows by SITC product-group 50
Table 12 Commodity pattern of trade in manufactures, 1929–1959 (by value) 50
Table 13 Commodity pattern of trade in manufacturers, 1929–1959 (by weight) 51

Table 14 Structure of intra-OECD imports and exports by SITC product-group 52
Table 15 Percent intra-OECD Exports/percent intra-OECD Imports, by SITC product-group 53
Table 16 Export shares 1963–1965 55
Table 17 Export shares 1971–1973 56
Table 18 Normalized export shares 1963–1965 57
Table 19 Normalized export shares 1971–1973 58
Table 20 Relative R&D-intensities of export patterns 59
Table 21 Relative R&D-intensities of export patterns (intra-EEC exports excluded) 60
Table 22 Spearman rank correlation coefficients of R&D-intensities correlated with measures of trading performance 68
Table 23 Rankings of trading performance and R&D-intensity 74
Table A.1 Assumed correspondence between ISIC, SITC and OECD R&D classifications 90
Table A.2 R&D expenditures (company-funded): 1967 94
Table A.3 R&D expenditures (company-funded): 1967. Disaggregated according to our estimates 95
Table A.4 R&D expenditures (company-funded): 1967 @ 1962 currency exchange rates, Freeman and Young RER applied, 1963 constant prices 98
Table A.5 Averaged R&D-intensities: 1967, 1969, 1971. 100
Table B.1 Normalized ratios of export differences (R_D) 105
Table B.2 Exports 1963–1965 107
Table B.3 Exports 1971–1973 108
Table B.4 Ratios of export shares (r_S) 111
Table B.5 Normalized ratios of export shares (R_S) 112

PREFACE

No one would deny the immense influence that technical change has had on economic development in the twentieth century. And yet it is only comparatively recently that economists have made any serious effort to bring technical change into their theoretical discussions, and to escape from the abstractions that have for so long bedeviled the mainstream of economic theory.

As regards international trade theory, the major step in this direction dates from the 1960s—the development of the technology gap and product-cycle theories. Industrial innovation was acknowledged as being an important source of comparative advantage in large areas of the modern industrial economy.

These theories have been accepted with surprisingly little argument in academic circles. As will be the main contention of this book, there are a number of important respects in which they are unsatisfactory in their present form. In particular, they were constructed (and tested) without recourse to detailed technological information, which led their exponents to underestimate the ability of the innovator to maintain and extend his monopoly power in the marketplace; and they failed to capture the dynamic impact of successful innovation on the location of production and the growth of industrial wealth.

Two limitations of this study should be noted: the analysis relates chiefly to the postwar historical period up to 1973, and especially to the decade 1963–1973, so that care should be taken in extrapolating to present-day economic conditions; and attention is concentrated on the most advanced industrial economies in the OECD—the problems of the less-developed countries are beyond the scope of the study.

Chapter I contains an introductory review of international trade theory. Chapter II takes a closer look at the theories that have been developed to take account of industrial innovation, the major part being a critique of the product-cycle theory. This is followed in Chapter III by a brief description of changes in patterns of international trade since World War II; in preparation for Chapter IV, in which a statistical analysis is carried out to assess the impact of product and process innovation on the historical trading performance of the industries under consideration. Methodological and statistical problems arising out of the need to measure (and compare across countries) innovative effort and trading performance are discussed in the Appendices.

I am grateful to the Programmes Analysis Unit, a joint unit of the Department of Industry, and the United Kingdom Atomic Energy Authority for the grant in 1975 that made this work possible. Various members of the Science Policy Research Unit have given me valuable advice during the course of the research, in particular Charles Cooper, Ray Curnow, Christopher Freeman, Paul Gardiner, Keith Pavitt, Roy Rothwell, and Luc Soete. I owe a special debt to Charles Cooper and Paul Gardiner for their criticisms of earlier drafts of this paper; to Miss Petrine McDonald for her help with data collection; and to Miss Sylvia Richards and Miss Sian Thomas for their secretarial assistance.

University of Sussex

Chapter I

Theories of International Trade

Three related branches of trade theory are usually distinguished in the literature: welfare theory—which sets out to predict the effects on economic welfare of free trade, autarchy, and the various intermediate positions dictated by tariff barriers and other trading restrictions; the theory associated with relationships between international trade and economic structure—which considers origins of comparative advantage and the "optimal" international allocation of resources between alternative types of production; and balance of payments theory—which deals with such questions as the elasticities of imports and exports to changes in currency exchange rates and to changes in national and international levels of demand. In this section we shall be concerned with the second of these themes.

RICARDIAN AND HECKSCHER-OHLIN TRADE MODELS

Before Ricardo, natural resources were regarded as the principal determinants of international trading patterns. Providence had granted the American colonies the climate and soil appropriate to growing cotton in large quantities, just as Britain had been endowed with ample supplies of coal. These natural "monopolies" were exploited as a matter of course to purchase other desirable commodities not available domestically. International trade involved exchanges of natural resources, or of manufactured goods dependent on their geographical proximity.

Ricardo recognized that other factors of production besides land contributed to comparative advantage, and hence to trade.[1] If relative prices of manufactured goods differed in the absence of trade, an exchange of goods could bring about an increase in economic welfare (in terms of real income) to both parties[2] Hence the attraction of trading manufactured goods internationally rather than relying entirely on domestic production to satisfy home demand. According to Ricardo, the relative prices of commodities varied from country to country due to differences in production costs, and production costs were in turn dominated by labor costs. Relative labor productivity thus became the principal determinant of comparative advantage. Disparaties in labor productivity were attributed by Ricardo to differences in production technology, although the origins of these disparities were unspecified.

In its attitudes toward production technology the next major development in trading theory—the so-called Heckscher-Ohlin theory (dating from the 1930s)—represented a move in the wrong direction.[3] To allow analytical simplicity, technology was assumed to be static and the common property of all nations. Technological disparities were no longer the source of relative price differences. And as in other branches of neoclassical economics, technology was regarded in the abstract as that which determined mathematical relationships (production functions) between factors of production (in this case labor) and their economic outputs. Technologies so defined were assumed to be independent of one another and unchanging.

The novelty of the Heckscher-Ohlin model lay in its inclusion of a second factor of production—capital. Price structures vary from country to country due to differing national endowments of capital and labor. A relatively capital-abundant country (e.g., the United States) will have a price advantage in capital-intensive goods which it will export in exchange for labor-intensive goods from a labor-abundant country (e.g., Mexico).[4] In the two-commodity idealization normally used by neoclassical economists to derive their theorems, trade will proceed once barriers are removed until commodity prices are equalized between the two countries. Endowments of capital and labor will be reallocated between production of the two commodities (e.g., food and clothing) to achieve this effect. Commodity prices are not the only variables that will be equalized. The "factor-price equalization" theorem predicts that, given free trade and equivalent technologies, wage rates and rentals on capital equipment (i.e., factor prices) will tend to converge internationally.[5]

The Heckscher-Ohlin model predicts factor reallocations that will take place following the resumption of trade between two countries; it also predicts reallocations arising from exogenous changes in factor endowments and commodity prices. Thus the Rybczynski theorem predicts that an increase in the endowment of one factor of production will increase the output of the commodity using that factor intensively and reduce the output of the other commodity.[6]

Before discussing the tests to which the neoclassical theory has been submitted, it is as well to spell out the principal assumptions upon which the theory in its *original* form was based, as they have become the focus for subsequent dissatisfaction:

—Technology is static (or if any change takes place it is exogenous to production), and countries have equal access to technical know-how.
—Labor and capital are completely mobile within the boundaries of the nation-state (the process of substituting one for the other is frictionless and has zero social cost), but completely immobile internationally.
—Labor is homogeneous in quality, nationally and internationally: it is equally skilled, equally entrepreneurial, equally devoted to hard work, and fully employed. Labor also has perfect knowledge of opportunities which it exploits to the full.
—Rankings of commodities according to factor-intensities of production are identical across countries, irrespective of factor price variations (e.g., in all countries production of food is more labor-intensive than production of clothing).
—Industries operate in climates of perfect competition and free trade; the doctrine of laissez-faire prevails.
—Relationships between inputs and outputs are independent of the scale of production: all industries experience constant returns to scale.
—Consumer preferences are identical across countries, and are determined solely by relative prices.
—Countries are assumed to employ their factors of production with equal efficiency; e.g., historical barriers to efficient utilization are not recognized.

TESTING THE NEOCLASSICAL TRADE MODEL

Any model developed by the social scientist to describe and predict behavior in the real world is bound to involve fairly drastic simplifications. The modeler's ambition is to capture the essential mechanisms driving the part of the social system he is depicting (if they exist), to the extent that the act of simplification or abstraction involves a relatively unimportant loss of explanatory power. The range of problems to which his model may be applied depends ultimately on his simplifying assumptions. As is apparent from the neoclassical assumptions listed above, economic modeling is not a value-free exercise.

Perhaps the most drastic simplification resorted to in the derivation of the Ricardian and Heckscher-Ohlin models involved reducing the world economy to distinct pairs of countries (or regions) exchanging distinct pairs of commodities. Conceiving trade in these terms has some validity, provided trade in the real world is predominantly bilateral.[7] Attempts have been made to extend the theory to encompass multilateral trade, but without marked success.[8] In contexts where multilateral trade predominates and the reduction to a bilateral model is impossible, the neoclassical theory is essentially untestable, and loses its explanatory and predictive power.

The two-commodity simplification is even more drastic, given that international trade involves the exchange of thousands of commodities of great variety (soap, automobiles, transformers, machine tools. . . .), both in character and in the factor-intensities of production. Neoclassicists have usually chosen "food" and "clothing" as their typical commodities, and have assumed that price alone determines consumer preference. In this and other respects, we shall see later that food and clothing, as conceived by the neoclassicists, are poorly representative of the bulk of present-day trade. In assuming commodities to be distinct, the neoclassicists also failed to capture the interdependence of products and technologies in the modern economy.

The above is not intended to give the impression that the Heckscher-Ohlin model is worthless. The point to emphasize is that it is limited in its applicability. Empirical tests of the model are summarized by Caves and Jones (1973).[9] It is evident that in certain localized contexts (especially where differences, or changes, in factor endowments are clear-cut) and for certain commodities, the neoclassical theory has given insights into economic developments. Furthermore, the model has proved capable of extension to take account of such "imperfections" as tariff barriers, imperfect competition, and nonconstant returns of scale, although predictions have again rested on the assumption of bilateral trade and distinct commodity pairs.[10]

THE LEONTIEF PARADOX

The most famous test of the Heckscher-Ohlin theory concerned the structure of U.S. trade. In 1953, Leontief demonstrated that the Heckscher-Ohlin model's predictions of the factor intensities of U.S. imports and exports were incorrect. Contrary to expectations, U.S. exports were more labor-intensive than U.S. imports.[11] This discovery led to some important entensions to the conventional trade theory, the debate revolving around the validity of the neoclassicists' assumptions. The most important explanations of the paradox are listed below.

Labor Skills

The hypothesis put forward by Leontief himself to explain the apparent paradox he had uncovered involved disparities in labor skills. He suggested that superior organizational ability resulted in more efficient use of labor in the United States than elsewhere in the world economy. For a given amount of capital, U.S. labor could be made twice as productive as its foreign counterpart.

Leontief's explanation has been discarded by most economists, although a satisfactory test has not been found. If U.S. management is a superior organizer of labor, would it not be an equally superior organizer of capital, in which case the hypothesis would be nullified? It has, however, been pointed out that if a distinction is drawn between endowments of skilled and unskilled labor, Leontief's paradox can be reversed. Relative to other coutnries, the United States is well endowed in skilled labor. Studies have confirmed that U.S. exports are "skilled-labor-intensive," whereas U.S. production of import-competing goods are "unskilled-labor-intensive."[12]

Factor-Intensity Reversals

We noted above that a key assumption of the Heckscher-Ohlin model referred to the rankings of commodities according to their factor intensities—the assumption being that rankings are everywhere identical. This stemmed partly from the additional assumption that technological knowledge was equally available to all producers. But what happens if food production is capital-intensive relative to textile production in one country, but labor-intensive relative to textiles in another country? Import-competing production in the first country would register as relatively capital-intensive, while imports themselves would be relatively labor-intensive—a potential source of error in Leontief's calculations.[13]

Empirical studies have confirmed that factor-intensity reversals do occur in the real world, especially between developed and underdeveloped countries. Most frequent are reversals in agricultural production (U.S. agriculture is highly capital-intensive), which go some way to explain the paradoxical trading patterns which have been observed for other countries besides the United States (e.g., India).

Resource Endowments

Leontief has been criticized for excluding the influence of the third factor of production—land—from his calculations. Over the last century, the United States has become more and more dependent on imports of "land-intensive" goods—goods dependent on abundant local supplies of natural resources—as the costs of exploiting depleted local stocks have increased. Resource-intensive goods being predominantly capital-intensive, this will introduce a bias into the factor-intensities of U.S. trading patterns.

Consumer Preference

The Ricardian and Heckscher-Ohlin predictions are deduced from a model based on an economy's capacity to supply certain goods given certain endowments of factors of production and technology; demand patterns are assumed to be identical from country to country. The anti-Leontief argument here is that the hunger of U.S. citizens for capital-intensive goods so occupies U.S. production that industry is unable to export the quantity of capital-intensive goods proportionate to its comparative advantage. Tests of this thesis have been inconclusive.

Technology Gap and Product Cycle

The technology gap and product-cycle theories have arguably been the most important by-product of Leontief's paradox. For the first time, technology was treated in trade theory as an endogenous variable, as something rather more concrete than the neoclassicists' determinant of production functions, and as an entity that was only mobile under certain conditions and (possibly) at certain stages of its development. The "neo-technology" theories (as they are frequently referred to) recognize that strong pressures exist within modern economies encouraging firms (and governments) to pursue technical change actively in order to gain or maintain competitive advantage; hence the large expenditures on industrial research and development in the major Western economies. This implies that in some contexts movement in the direction of disequilibrium rather than equilibrium is the "natural" economic tendency—in contradiction to a central tenet of neoclassical economics.

The neo-technology theories and their implications will be discussed at some length in the next section. An additional attraction of these theories should be noted in passing: they avoid four of the crucial and most criticized assumptions of the neoclassical model—that labor skills are everywhere identical, that capital and labor are mobile only within national boundaries, that industries operate in conditions of perfect competition, and that industries experience constant returns to scale.

Redefining "Capital" and "Labor"

Economists have argued that the Leontief paradox can be reconciled with the neoclassical trade theory by redefining the terms "capital" and labor—"provided that 'capital' is conceived of in the broad sense as comprising natural resources, social capital, human skills, and technological and organisational knowledge, as well as material capital equipment, while 'labour' is conceived of in the analytically relevant narrow sense of human time availability only, instead of being identified broadly with all the services to production rendered through human beings."[14] High technology, skilled-labor-intensive products in which U.S. industry specializes would therefore be reclassified as "capital"-intensive, reconfirming the Heckscher-Ohlin predictions of the net capital-intensity of U.S. exports. Again, we shall be returning to these arguments in a later context.

OTHER THEORIES OF INTERNATIONAL TRADE

Two further theories explaining trading patterns deserve mention—the one concerned with scale economies, the other with relationships between income levels and consumer preferences.

Scale Economies

Countries possessing large home markets with correspondingly high purchasing power will specialize in commodities benefiting from increasing returns to the scale of production. Tariff barriers, uncertain foreign markets and transport costs will discourage the small country from producing these goods (although the threat of dependence on monopoly supply of strategic goods may encourage government intervention).

An extension of this theme has been suggested by Drèze (1960). The extent of product differentiation in international markets influences the degree to which small countries can use exports to exact scale economies. If a product is internationally standardized (e.g., copper tubing), a small country can benefit from scale economies. However, if products are internationally differentiated (especially if differentiation is "frozen" by trademarks), possibly as a result of different tastes and traditions, manufacturers serving large domestic markets will have greater opportunities for exploiting scale economies—and for imposing their tastes on their neighbors (e.g., Colgate toothpaste). Large countries will thus have a comparative advantage in the production of differentiated goods. Drèze used the structure of Belgian trade to test his hypothesis, and found a reasonably good level of explanation.

Income Levels and Consumer Preferences

An important challenge to the neoclassical theory has come from Linder (1961). According to Linder, consumer preference is closely associated with income level: as incomes rise, consumers will demand an increasing variety of goods. In a low-income economy, majority demand will be concentrated on food, clothing, and a relatively narrow selection of household goods. In a high-income economy, demand will exist for a much greater variety of goods, of very variable sophistication.

On the supply side, entrepreneurs will set up production in goods for which there is a clearly discernible economic need, and that is most likely to be detected within the economy with which they are most familiar—the domestic economy.[15] If his enterprise is successful domestically, the time will come when the home economy is unable to provide sufficient opportunities for growth, so that he will seek markets abroad to satisfy ambitions.

As Linder was able to demonstrate (and see Chapter III below), demand internal to an economy normally absorbs the great majority of home production. He argued that exports should be regarded essentially as "overspill." In his own words, "international trade is really nothing but an extension across national frontiers of a country's own web of economic activity."[16] Demand patterns (and hence industrial structures and commodities produced) being equivalent in countries with equivalent per capita income levels, these countries will tend to trade more intensively with one another than with countries possessing either higher or lower income levels.[17]

It should be noted that Linder's hypothesis is in complete opposition to a central prediction of the Heckscher-Ohlin model—that the greater the disparities in capital and labor endowments between countries, the greater the opportunities for trade. If capital accumulation is positively correlated with income level (a reasonable assumption), the neoclassical theory predicts that trade should be most intensive between countries with different income levels.[18]

A difficulty with Linder's hypothesis that he himself was unable to explain satisfactorily is as follows: if countries with similar proportions of labor and capital produce similar commodities, where is the source of comparative advantage that generates trade? If monopoly gained via specialization is the source, does this not contradict the initial assumption that countries with similar income levels have similar commodity compositions of production?[19] Can product differentiation *within* a product group provide an explanation? We shall return to these important questions in another context. There are other valid reasons for being dissatisfied with Linder's model: he understated the tendency for underdeveloped countries to be single-commodity producers (e.g., Ghana in cocoa, Argentina in meat) which they may trade intensively with high-income countries, but hardly at all between themselves; he overlooked the manner in which rich minority groups with Western tastes tend to dominate demand in underdeveloped countries; he failed to take account of capital mobility. Nevertheless, Linder's model remains important, and is probably capable of further useful extension.

WHICH THEORY?

If the Linder and neoclassical models are diametrically opposed, and neither has been emphatically refuted when empirically tested, where are we placed with regard to our understanding of international trade (assuming for the moment that the tests have been adequate)? This quandary only arises if the ambition is to seek a holistic explanation of trading phenomena. That such an explanation will ever exist is of course a false hope. Given the tremendous range of forces that can influence trading patterns, our understanding must necessarily consist of a patchwork of theories, their validity depending entirely on the context to which they are applied.

An important paper by Hufbauer (1970) supports this viewpoint. He set out to test the degree to which various theories explained the import and export patterns of twenty-four Western countries, and concluded that each theory survived unscathed. In his own words, there appeared to be "a little truth in every nook." However, each theory had its set of trading problems that it was particularly adept at solving. Thus, in the confrontation between Linder and neoclassical orthodoxy,

> Linder—perhaps supplemented by product cycle and scale economy theory—works best in accounting for trade *within* the rich country zone. By the same token, orthodoxy . . . does better at explaining the commodity composition of manufacture *within* the poor country zone. As for trade between zones, the . . . results agree with Linder if the zones are close together, and with orthodoxy when the zones are widely separated.

The problem thus becomes one of demarcation—distinguishing areas in which variables and assumptions embodied in disparate theories are most likely to be influential.

NOTES

1. Classical and neoclassical models of international trade are discussed at length by Bhagwati (1968) and Caves and Jones (1973).

2. Relative price: the quantity of one commodity that may be exchanged for a unit of another commodity.

3. In the century preceding the Heckscher-Ohlin model, Ricardo's ideas were greatly refined, especially by J. S. Mill and Alfred Marshall. The latter's contribution, the development of analytical techniques for determining "equilibrium" terms of trade, was especially influential.

4. The Heckscher-Ohlin model can also be extended to incorporate relative abundance of the third traditional factor of production—land—although with some difficulty. For obvious reasons, the assumption of homogeneity is even less applicable to land than it is to labor or capital, so that "relative land-abundance" tends to be meaningless without qualitative description.

5. This theorem is also crucially dependent on the assumption that labor and capital cannot cross national boundaries. If they could freely (so that relative abundances were evened out), there would presumably be no further source of competitive advantages and all trade would cease.

6. See Caves and Jones (1973) for a discussion of this and other theorems predicting reactions to price and endowment changes.

7. In analyzing the structure of a particular country's imports and exports, trade is sometimes regarded as bilateral between the country and the "rest of the world." This approach requires great caution, assuming as it does international homogeneity of factor endowments and tariffs, and complete mobility of capital and labor in the "rest of the world."

8. Hansson (1952), devised a model incorporating three regions, which he characterized according to the abundance or scarcity of land, labor or capital. Although he claimed a good level of explanation of pre-World War I trading behavior, it has proved inapplicable beyond certain rather narrow contexts.

9. Pp. 192–195.

10. A more fundamental criticism of neoclassical economics relates to the problems of measuring capital. The neoclassical model is constructed on the assumption that labor and capital can be valued independently. But, to quote Harcourt (1972), "it is impossible to conceive of a quantity of 'capital in general,' the value of which is independent of the rates of interest and wages." While argument has raged around this point since the early 1950s, alternative models put forward by the critics appear little more related to "real world" economic conditions than their predecessors.

11. Leontief's method was ingenious: he calculated the quantities of labor and capital used in the production of a million dollars' worth of U.S. exports and compared them with the quantities used in producing a million dollars' worth of

import-competing goods. He made use of recently compiled input-output tables of the U.S. economy to include labor and capital costs incurred upstream of final assembly (e.g., capital inputs by the steel industry into steel plate used in the shipyards). Factor inputs to import-competing production rather than to straight imports had to be considered in the absence of internationally comparable statistics. See Leontief (1953). By applying Leontief's method to the trading patterns of other countries, economists have revealed further apparent paradoxes. Thus Indian exports to the United States have been shown to be more capital-intensive than Indian goods produced in competition with imports from the United States.

12. E.g., Baldwin (1971).

13. See Minhas (1962).

14. Johnson (1968), Second Lecture, p. 1. This is clearly an extension of the labor skills argument outlined above.

15. Similarly, the inventor of a new product will be motivated by needs perceived within his own country.

16. Linder (1961), p. 88.

17. Linder suggested that "distance factors"—transport costs, different languages, unfamiliarity with foreign markets—will result in less than perfect exploitation of opportunities, especially between underdeveloped countries.

18. The Heckscher-Ohlin model is concerned almost entirely with the supply of goods. Attempts to build demand (and consumer preferences) into the model have brought it into closer agreement with Linderism (see Meade, 1952).

19. Linder undoubtedly made life difficult for himself by overstating the tendency of income levels to result in equivalent industrial structures. Sweden and Germany may be cited as countries with approximately similar per capita incomes, but very distinct industrial specializations.

Chapter II

Technology Gap and Product Cycle Theories

As we have seen, the neoclassical theory of international trade is based on the assumptions that technology is unchanging and is equally available to all countries. The technology gap and product cycle theories set out to explain trading behavior in manufacturing industries where these assumptions are least applicable—industries in which technological innovation plays an important part in industrial competition and the location of comparative advantage. In this chapter we shall first summarize these theories and the tests to which they have been submitted, and then devote some space to criticism.

TECHNOLOGY-GAP MODEL

The Technology-Gap model was first proposed by Posner (1961). Suppose that a company develops a completely new product in reaction to a perceived market demand, and that the market responds favorably to the innovation. As demand grows, threatened companies, at home and abroad, react by attempting to imitate the new product.

Imitation takes time, and during the years that the innovating company maintains its monopoly control over the technology, it gains a strong hold on national and international markets. A one-way flow of exports builds up from the innovating country. Sooner or later, however, competitors' efforts at imitation are rewarded, and the original innovator's market expansion is checked. If an overseas industry imitates successfully and has cheaper factors of production at its disposal, comparative advantage may well be reversed, and the innovating country will become a net importer of the product, while the imitator becomes a net exporter.

Scale economies play an important part in the model. While the ball is in his court, the innovator, faced by rapidly expanding demand, can afford to risk erecting large plants, expecting to benefit from static economies of scale. Overseas competitors may thus remain at a price disadvantage despite lower labor costs. Similarly with production learning effects (dynamic scale economies). Assuming that production knowledge is a function of the length of time an industry has been producing a particular product, the imitator will enter at a disadvantage; teething troubles can only be overcome as experience accumulates. Scale economies generally prolong the life and increase the volume of technology-gap exports.

PRODUCT-CYCLE THEORY

An extended version of the technology-gap theory was developed by Hirsch (1965) and Vernon (1966).[1] They argued that the location of production depended not so much on the extent to which competitors succeeded in imitating a new product as on the characteristics of production associated with the product at the different stages of its "lifetime."

The product-cycle theory was developed primarily with a view to explaining U.S. trading behavior. According to Vernon, the United States is a fertile source of innovations for two reasons: the high income level, which generates demand for a wide variety of sophisticated goods (reminiscent of Linder); and the scarcity of labor and abundance of capital which encourages the search for labor-saving devices.[2,3] U.S. entrepreneurs will tend to be the first to react to these opportunities, having greatest knowledge of their own market.

The product-cycle thesis is summarized in Figure 1. In the early stages, the technology is unstable and changing rapidly; opinion is divided as to the best technical configuration, and much experimental work (and in some cases scientific explanation) is required before a relatively "stable" product emerges. The strength and nature of market demand is also very uncertain. At this stage, scientific and engineering ability are crucial to survival, and the firm will tend to lean on other specialist firms to supply components and materials, rather than tying

Figure 1

Characteristics of Product Cycle

Characteristics	Product-Cycle Phase		
	Early	Growth	Mature
Technology	Short runs Rapidly changing techniques Dependence on external economies	Mass production methods gradually introduced Variations in techniques still frequent	Long runs and stable technnology Few innovations of importance
Capital intensity	Low	High, due to high obsolescence rate	High, due to large quantity of specialised equipment
Industry structure	Entry is know-how determined Numerous firms providing specialised services	Growing number of firms Many casualties and mergers Growing vertical integration	Financial resources critical for entry Number of firms declining
Critical human inputs	Scientific and engineering	Management	Unskilled and semi-skilled labor
Demand structure	Sellers' market Performance and price of substitute determine buyers' expectations	Individual producers face growing price elasticity Intra-industry competition reduces prices Product information spreading	Buyers' market Information easily available

Source: Hirsch (1965).

up capital in production facilities that may rapidly become outdated.

Thus, for a period after the innovation, production remains in the parent country; close contact with specialist suppliers upstream (allowing the innovator to change his inputs easily) and an uncertain market downstream outweigh the benefits that might accrue from exploiting cheaper factors of production overseas. Furthermore, monopolistic control results in a low price elasticity of demand for the new product—within limits, the producer can fix prices without being too concerned by his competitors' production costs. After a time, however, as demand for the product accelerates at home and abroad, a tendency to standardize both the product and its associated production processes becomes more evident. As mass production is introduced, relative production costs and scale economies grow in importance. The advantages of serving foreign markets from domestic headquarters diminish, profitability decreases, and pressures increase to set up production facilities in lower-cost locations. The market share of the original innovator is increasingly threatened as competitors at home and abroad imitate and improve the new product.

Vernon went to some lengths to emphasize the variety of forces that may influence the timing of the transfer of production from the parent country: tariff barriers, transport costs, and the behavior of competitors may induce the manufacturer to invest abroad earlier or later than would otherwise be expected. Such decisions are unlikely even to be particularly rational, based as they inevitably are on "guestimates" of future competitive conditions. A clear trend toward direct investment overseas will, however, become apparent on examining an adequate sample of products.

In the final stage of the product cycle, the market is well known and the product standardized. Mass-production techniques prevail, and production costs are the dominant influences on comparative advantage. Little innovation beyond superficial product differentiation takes place, and external economies will have decreased in significance. The original innovating country will most likely have become a net importer of the standardized product. Hence the product-cycle theory's explanation of the Leontief paradox. The product cycle is characterized by a movement from labor-intensity to relative capital intensity as the product "matures." The United States will tend to export products at a labor-intensive stage of production, and import them once they have become relatively capital-intensive.

As Vernon points out, the transfer of relatively capital-intensive production to countries typically abundant in labor but scarce in capital might appear to contradict the Heckscher-Ohlin theorem—replacing one paradox (Leontief's) with another. He suggested three explanations: the stability of the market for standardized products encourages countries poorly endowed with marketing expertise (or at a distance from large markets) to specialize in such goods; the innovating industries may transfer their own capital to the labor-abundant country, eager to extract the maximum possible production cost savings from the cheap labor supply (remember that the transferred industry may still be labor-intensive by the standards of the innovating country—e.g., television assembly); and "imperfections" in the capital markets of the capital-scarce country (e.g., government investment grants) may provide sufficiently cheap capital to encourage production that is capital-intensive relative to the norm of the country in question.

If capital and labor are redefined as suggested by Johnson, the product cycle may be seen in another light, as involving the gradual replacement of one form of capital—that embodied in labor skills and technical knowledge—for another—that embodied in capital equipment. In which case, countries deficient in the former will be barred from production until standardization drastically reduces its significance, whereafter they will have a distinct comparative advantage. The product cycle is accompanied by diminishing *innovational* entry costs.

VALIDITY OF THE NEO-TECHNOLOGY THEORIES

The Technology-Gap Theory: Tests

The technology-gap thesis was the subject of a series of studies carried out in the 1960s. Freeman (1963) and Hufbauer (1965) looked at technology-gap trade in the plastics and synthetic-fiber industries, Freeman (1965) and Hirsch (1965) examined the electronic industries, and the OECD conducted a number of studies of different industries—e.g., drugs and computers. The focus for attention throughout was the technology gap that had allegedly opened up between the United States and Western Europe after World War II. In general, the OECD studies concentrated on the evidence (qualified manpower, R&D expenditures, first commercial exploitation . . .) for the existence of technology gaps, rather than on testing the theory per se. More recently, the possible existence of "reverse" technology gaps between Europe and the United States has caused concern in the United States [Boretsky (1969)], and a number of studies have been carried out estimating technology gaps between the United States and the USSR [OECD (1969)].

The more rigorous tests of the technology-gap theory, especially that by Hufbauer (1965), have provided a reasonably high degree of confirmation. The methodology is fairly standard: at the micro-level, examine the development of production in selected *radical* innovations (we shall have more to say about the concentration on radical innovations below); at the macro-level, examine trade flows over time in selected product groups. In his study of the plastics and synthetic-fiber industries, Hufbauer demonstrated that:

—Distinct lags were detectable between production in country A (the "innovator") and in country B (the "imitator"), although the length of the time-lag was very variable from product to product. For instance, the intervals between the inventions of polymethyl methacrylate and Galalith in Germany and their first commercial production in the United Kingdom, were three and fifteen years, respectively.

—There was evidence (in some products) of early exporters later becoming importers (Germany and Galalith), and of *some* low-wage countries becoming net exporters after a slow process of import substitution (Italy and Celluloid).

—The size of home markets significantly influenced the direction of synthetic materials trade (via static scale economies), although this influence was probably exaggerated by tariff barriers.

As is apparent from the above, the technology-gap theory's main shortcoming was a rather naive view of the mechanisms behind the transfer of production from one country to another; imitation was overemphasized, capital mobility (and monopoly powers) underemphasized. As a consequence, the theory lacks precision in its prediction of the *timing* and *direction* (to which countries) of production transfers. It was to these problems that Vernon addressed himself in his more detailed product-cycle hypothesis.

The Product-Cycle Theory: Tests

Surprisingly, the product-cycle theory remains inadequately tested, even though it was first elaborated ten years ago. Vernon admitted in his 1966 paper that his ideas were little more than speculations, requiring thorough testing before they could be elevated to the rank of established theory. Unfortunately, Vernon's hypotheses are all too often accepted as proven (with a few reservations); what is worse, the technology-gap studies which preceded the 1966 paper are frequently cited as corroborations of his theory, rather than as providers of puzzles which stimulated his reinterpretation. And the "recognized" tests of the theory (Hirsch, Stobaugh, Wells . . .) cannot be regarded as conclusive as they neglect to look *at a technological level* at the manner in which products and processes change over time.

Two groups of questions are crucial to any assessment of Vernon's theory. The first concerns the alleged historical tendency toward stability and standardization of products and their associated production processes and markets. Is this tendency sufficiently widespread to allow generalization, and to be discernible in macro-economic trends? Is stabilization a feature of some product groups, but not of others? If so, why do some products (and production processes and markets) stabilize, while others do not? The second concerns the degree of monopoly control that an innovator can retain over his innovation. To what extent do patents and other monopolistic devices allow the innovator to control the transfer of production, and to render imitation impossible? Is monopoly control easier to exert in some industries (and markets) than in others? Can the assumption implicit in the product-cycle theory, namely, that the age of a product bears some relation to the extent of monopoly control, be substantiated, and for which products? As will become apparent, the issues of product stability and monopoly power have close links.

Once again, our task is one of demarcation: which (if any) product/industry groups conform to Vernon's thesis; which contradict it?

These questions will be the subject of our attention in the next three chapters. In the first, "product behavior" will be briefly described in an industry that does not appear to square with the product-cycle theory: textile machinery. It will be apparent that the essential characteristics of product development in this industry are to be found in many other modern industries. In the second and third, we shall consider industries which appear at first sight to fit the product-cycle description: chemicals and electronic consumer goods. It should be stressed that the following descriptions are overstatements, in the sense that diversity in competitive behavior within product groups is much greater than depicted. The intention is to identify characteristics that are predominant, but not necessarily found throughout the industry.

PRODUCT-CYCLE "NONCONFORMISTS": TEXTILE MACHINERY

First, a look at the market for textile machinery.[4] The textile industry remains, by the standards of the industrialized countries, a labor-intensive industry. With rising labor costs and shortages of skilled operatives, and faced by the constant threat of low-wage competition from Third World countries, there has been a strong and undiminishing demand for machinery offering substantial labor savings. Figure 2 demonstrates that the increase in productivity in the principal cotton industry processes has been dramatic since World War II, suggesting a high level of innovative activity in the textile machinery industry. Technical change has also been stimulated by the introduction of artificial fibers, which have opened up many new opportunities for the textile manufacturers, as well as posing many new problems.

The typical textile manufacturer operates a series of linked processes which transform the raw fibers into a knitted or woven fabric. In the cotton industry the main processes are: opening and cleaning, carding, drawing, roving, spinning, beaming, warp-sizing, and weaving. The art is to maintain a continuous and profitable flow through the system. Advances in one process have tended to accentuate the demand for productivity increases (and quality improvements) in neighboring processes—to preserve balance and to avoid the emergence of bottlenecks.

The textile machinery industry typically is comprised of small and medium-sized specialist firms. Although these firms are numerous, it is usual that a very small number compete world-wide for a particular specialist market. Batch-production is normal.

Given the thirst for labor-saving devices in the textile industry, it is not surprising that product innovation has been central to competition between the machinery manufacturers. A common pattern in product development is as follows. In response to market demands, a firm perceives

Figure 2
Productivity Developments in Principal Cotton Industry Processes, 1900–1965

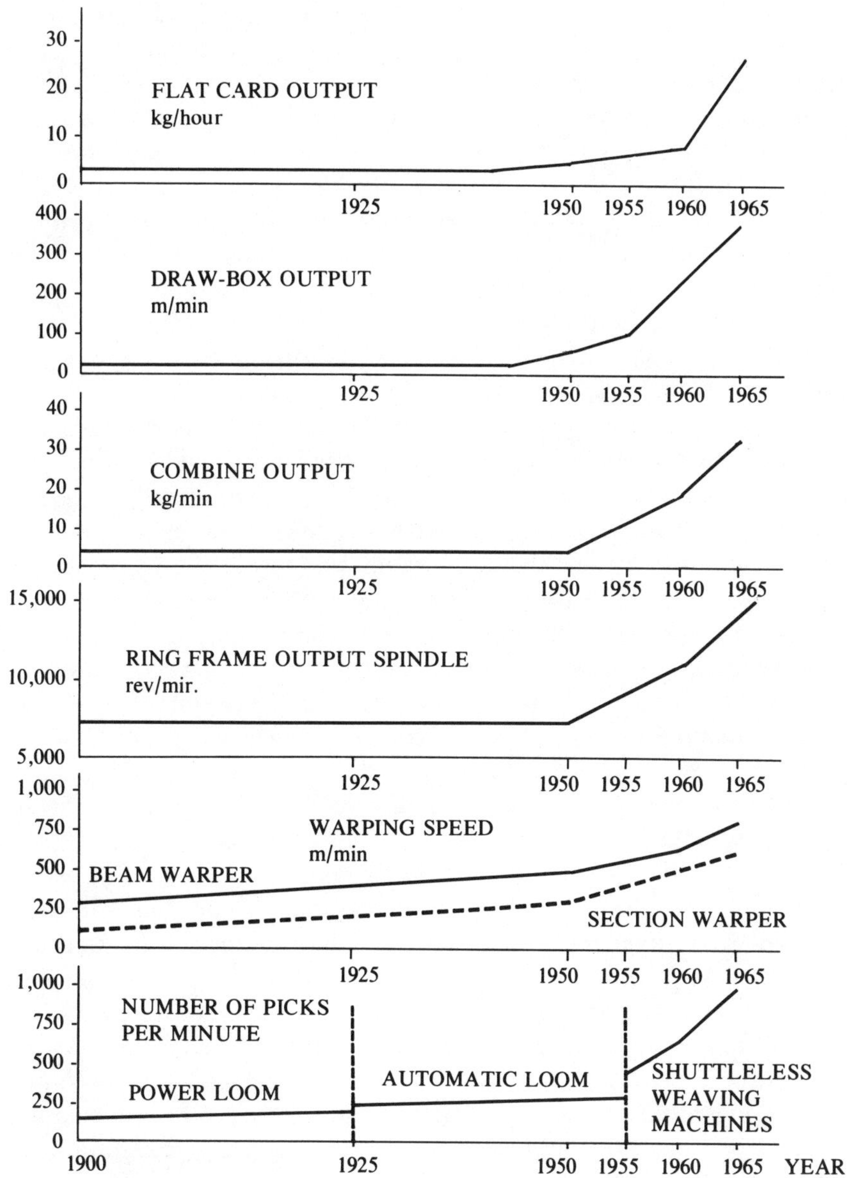

Source: Figure 3 of T. Jedryka, "Principal Technical Development Trends in the Textile Industries," in UN, *Lodz Textile Seminars: 1 Textile Fibres,* New York, 1970. Cited by Shepherd (1974).

an opportunity for which it believes it has a technical solution and the necessary manufacturing expertise. A period of intense developmental activity, market assessment, and production planning follows, taking anything from a few months to several years, at the end of which time a new product is introduced to the market. If the product is commercially successful, threatened competitors will embark on an equally intense effort to catch up with, and overtake, the new product. In some cases, although they are probably exceptional, the innovation will represent such an advance (e.g., the Sulzer loom) that few will have the resources to offer any challenge, and the monopoly will be complete; they will be forced to divert their resources into other product lines.

Since World War II, textile machinery has become increasingly sophisticated, both in its design and manufacture.[5] Design requires expertise in various branches of mechanics, metallurgy, control systems, and even aerodynamics in the modern machine, as well as detailed knowledge of production problems in the textile industry—yarn strength, operator safety, and so on. Manufacture similarly requires a variety of expertise, in machining and assembly, organization and marketing. It is above all the *accumulation and extension* of design and production expertise by established firms that provides the main barrier to entry (or re-entry).

Even if a competitor in a low-wage country managed to develop a machine that dodged the patents and matched the performance characteristics of the first product of its type on the market, he would be unlikely to break the grip of the original innovator. Where production is highly skilled, dynamic scale economies (production learning) will significantly reduce production costs; and the imitator will be hampered by technical teething troubles that will by that time have been conquered by the earlier manufacturer. Most important, though, the technical leader will not have stood still while the storm clouds gathered; its R&D and design departments will have been engaged in developing the next model, or generation, of its original innovation, aided by the profit generated by the original innovation. By the time the opposition has succeeded in imitating, or even surpassing, mark 1, the leader will be preparing to bring mark 2 to the market.[6] Monopoly power is maintained by product improvement (which may itself involve major innovations), not by seeking low factor cost locations for production. The textile machinery industry is characterised by relative immobility of capital resources, and little product licensing.[7]

Product development is thus not unlike a game of leapfrog: firm A develops a machine with performance P_1, whereupon firms B and C develop machines with performance P_2 and P_3, by which time firm A has improved the performance of its machine to P_4. This proceeds until firm D comes up with a radically new concept—perhaps combining two production processes into one—which in turn becomes the focus for innovative attention.[8] Competing firms are acutely aware of their rivals' technical advances; imitation is widespread, but is only part of the strategy aimed at outdoing the innovator.

An important additional source of growth and influence for the innovating firm is to extend the range of the new product's applications. This may entail bringing out a series of models, all incorporating the new concept but designed to satisfy different markets (e.g., modifying the Sulzer loom to weave cotton, jute, synthetic fibers, synthetic tapes, or to weave different widths of cloth).

The rate at which the technology moves forwards and sideways naturally depends on conditions internal and external to the industry: the impatience of the market for labor-saving devices; levels of investment in both the textile and textile-machinery industries; the availability of fertile new ideas, components and materials from government laboratories, universities and industries upstream.[9]

This last point needs stressing. The term "footloose" has frequently been used to describe industries that are not dependent on nearby natural resource endowments for comparative advantage. The textile machinery industry could by this definition be described as footloose, while the food-processing industry could not. However, in another sense the textile machinery industry is definitely not a footloose industry; it benefits (on the supply side) from being part of a highly developed industrial infrastructure, in three respects. First, the skill-intensity of manufacture (and product development) requires a continuous supply of skilled manpower.[10] Second, the industry reaps external economies, and reduces risks, by subcontracting parts of its production to specialist firms (toolmakers, foundries, gear manufactures), with which it may have long-standing ties resulting in a mutual understanding of production problems. Third, the above-mentioned flow of novel ideas from upstream greatly eases the task of *sustaining* product development; a new alloy may confer a crucial advantage to the firm that first recognizes its potential.[11] For these reasons, only highly industrialized countries have the indigenous ability to sustain production in such skill-intensive manufacture.

Is there any evidence of product (and market and process) standardization, in Vernon's sense, taking place historically in this industry?[12] There does not appear to be. Technical change, at least since World War II, has been continuous and rapid.

In describing technical change as "continuous," we are perhaps guilty of exaggeration. It is more nearly correct to think of products advancing via a series of plateaus, and to recognize the existence (and necessity as far as the producer is concerned) of *generational* stability. Between the introduction of new models, the innovator will market a product that is temporarily stabilized; if this were not possible, uncertainties would be too great, production sequences too unsettled, and there would be little prospect for an adequate return on invested capital. There is no question of this leading in itself to a relocation of production, as the product (and its planned successor) remains firmly under the control of the innovator. In the textile machinery industry, the interval between successive generations of equipment is typically four years, the rhythm partly imposed by the four-yearly occurrence of the International Textile Machinery Exhibition.

So far, the impression may have been given that success in textile machinery manufacture depends entirely on the firm's ability to generate new technologies in reaction to perceived market demands. This is not the case. To survive, the firm must sell at prices attractive in the marketplace—demand is never totally price-insensitive, however unique the product—and to generate profits from its innovations. Factor costs and productive efficiency (broadly defined) are therefore far from being irrelevant. The firm also has to be able to muster and organize the human and financial resources it needs to penetrate and service world markets. Failure to expand productive capacity to meet demand effectively lowers entry (or re-entry) barriers facing competitors.

A series of case studies by Rothwell demonstrates that it is above all else the combination of innovativeness and high (and rapidly growing) productivity that provides the key to the location of comparative advantage in textile machinery manufacture. Take the case of the highly successful Belgian loom manufacturer Picanol Weefautomaten.[13] It has married its innovative efforts (which in this case have accompanied a deliberate strategy of following the leaders) with an "intensive application of the philosophy of increasing productivity." One aspect has been the attempt to design new machines to have the maximum number of parts in common with existing machines—innovative effort has been directed at both increasing performance and reducing production costs.[14] This form of internal standardization has allowed the firm to attain a high level of productive efficiency despite a broad range of machine types; it has helped customers to economize on stocks of spare parts; it has reduced Picanol's servicing and after-sales costs; and ironically it has also lowered the costs and risks attached to innovation—especially in relation to the costs of manufacturing start-up.

Having said this, it must be admitted that the interactions between a firm's overall economic performance (and expectations) and its propensity to innovate are little understood. Nevertheless, it should be clear by now that the model outlined above, incomplete though it may be, bears little resemblance to the Hirsch/Vernon product-cycle formulation. Referring back to Figure 1: *technology* is changing rapidly, is dependent throughout on external economies, and competitiveness can only be procured by sustained innovative effort *and* increase in productivity; *capital intensity* tends to be consistently high (especially in the Johnsonian sense); *industry structure* tends to be oligopolistic, and financial resources, know-how, and a supporting industrial infrastructure are required for successful entry; *critical human inputs* are scientific and engineering, managerial (including marketing and after-sales services) and skilled operatives throughout; and *demand structure* tends to be characterized by relative price inelasticity.

It is not only in the textile machinery industry that "out-innovating" competitors is necessary for survival; the need to develop new *and* improved products is, if anything, even more pressing in other advanced "systems technology" industries—especially aircraft, heavy electrical machinery, computers, nuclear energy, specialist machine tools, and scientific instruments. This is especially the case where governments have intervened for military or other reasons to force the pace of technical change. Unfortunately, there is not the space here to describe product behavior in these industries, but a glance at the literature is sufficient to convince the reader that product stability is very exceptional (although generational stability is typical).[15] The product-cycle theory would appear to have poor explanatory power in a very substantial segment of the modern industrial state.

Figure 3

Shearer-Loader Development 1954 – 1973

	1954 – 1957	1958 – 1961
Anderson (Strathclyde) (U.K.)	Low seam drum shearer Vertical drum shearer Compressed air shearer Shuttle shearer Multi-disc cutter loader Type 16/80 hp Pickaback	16/100 hp 16/125 hp Trepan-shearer Hollow-plow shearer Dranyam Double trepan-shearer 16/125 ranging overcut shearer 16/125 ranging drum shearer Bucket-drum shearer Mawco
Eickhoff (West Germany)	Scroll drum cutter loader WSE III Electrohydraulic 80 hp WSE IV Pickaback	Large pick plow shearer EDW 100 hp Ranging 2-arm 2-drum shearer Double fixed drum shearer Thin-seam shearer
British Jeffrey Diamond (U.K.)	70 hp Mechanical 70 hp Hydraulic Pickaback	Magnamatic 80 hp Ranging-head shearer 100 hp shearer Lump shearer Trepan shearer Magnamatic 125 hp Composite gearhead shearer 150 hp shearer Ranging-arm shearer
Shearer-Loader patents filed in U.K. (all sources)	30	54

Acronyms: DERDS — Double-ended ranging drum shearer; SERDS — Single-ended ranging drum shearer; FIDD — Fully-integrated double drum; WSE — Walzenschrammlader Eickhoff; EDW — Eickhoff Doppelwalzenschrammlader

Source: Townsend (1976).

Major Machines Introduced by Machinery Manufacturers

1962 – 1965	1966 – 1969	1970 – 1973
Angled fixed-drum shearer Bi-directional shearer 16/125 lump shearer Conveyor-mounted trepanner Thin-seam 60 hp Thin-seam 80 hp Double-ended conveyor-mounted trepanner 16/125 DERDS MK I & Venturi drum shearer 16/200 DERDS MK I & Ranging turret shearer	Rolf shearer FIDD boom-shearer Ranging double-ended shearer DERDs MK II Slow speed bi-directional 400 hp shearer 300 hp shearer	Ranging drum MK II Ripping ranging shearer Heading ranging shearer Ranging outboardarm shearer
SERDS Bi-directional shearer 200 hp DERDs Thin-seam MK II Screwdrum SERDS 'EKomatic' haulage shearer Screwdrum SERDS 200 EDW	130 hp EDW Doubledrum shearer	Thin-seam MK III EDW 270 hp SERDS EDW 270 hp DERDS Short-face shearer EDW 170 DERDS EDW 170 hp SERDS 400 hp shearer
Bi-directional shearer 50 hp Ranging-drum 200 hp shearer Minimatic	FIDD boom-shearer 200 hp DERDS 200 hp SERDS Rolf shearer Slow-speed bi-directional	Short-in-lane shearer 200 hp SERDS 200 hp Maximatic In Web shearer Ripping shearer 400 hp shearer
76	106	98

One final example from the mechanical engineering industry will add strength to the argument. Following the invention in 1952 of an important type of underground coal-mining machine (the Anderton shearer-loader), its manufacture has been dominated by three engineering firms—two British, one German.[16] Townsend (1976) has traced the evolution of this machine, which is summarized in Figure 3. The increase in machine capability between 1952 and 1973 was dramatic—achieved by the accumulation of major and minor innovations. Knowledge of shearer-loader technology is not needed to appreciate that Figure 3 presents quite a different picture of product development from that described by the product-cycle theorists.[17]

Above, we have depicted industries in which the pace of technical change has been particularly rapid. There is a danger of being drawn into exaggeration. In mechanical engineering, for instance, there are sectors (e.g., pneumatic tools, pumps and valves) where the rate of technical change was relatively slow in the 1960s—largely because of a lack of pressure from the market for new and improved machines—and where oligopolistic structures have survived for reasons other than their innovative capabilities. And in the machine-tool industry, there are some basic products (e.g., standard lathes) that have changed little technically since 1945, although their share of total machine-tool demand in the OECD has consistently declined as more specialized machinery has taken over. In the production of these basic machines, standardization has certainly assisted in the transfer of production to lower factor cost locations—to Spain, to Eastern Europe, to South America. Studies are needed to explain why some technologies in this industry have standardized, others have not.

Competitive behavior within the innovation-intensive industries identified above varies considerably in one important respect: the extent to which production and technology are transferred outside the parent country. As we have seen, the textile and coal-mining machinery industries are characterized by relative immobility of capital resources, although there are distinct differences in their attitudes toward licensing. The same applies to production in the civilian aircraft and nuclear industries. In contrast, the computer and instrument industries have witnessed fairly widespread if sporadic capital movements, predominantly in one direction: from the United States to Europe. There can be no tidy, "single-variable" explanation for these disparities in capital mobility; each industry has to be considered in its peculiar technological, economic, geographical, and political context. Each industry has its own structural characteristics, marketing problems, competitive pressures. Furthermore, each country has, at a particular moment in history, its own set of internal economic and political conditions encouraging or discouraging the movement of capital overseas, and its own problems in penetrating protected foreign markets (compare the U.S. and West German levels of foreign investment since World War II). The point we wish to stress here is that capital mobility has *not* been significantly inspired by an "inexorable" trend toward product standardization in these industries.[18,19]

PRODUCT-CYCLE "CONFORMISTS": CHEMICALS

A completely different product profile is typically to be found in the chemical industries. It would at first sight appear more in sympathy with the product-cycle theory, as the criterion of product stability following invention and an early period of uncertainty is generally satisfied.[20] A chemical product is strictly defined by its chemical structure; although improvements in production processes may, for example, increase the purity and homogeneity of the product, it is by most standards relatively stable. As such, the nomenclature "product-cycle" is here rather inappropriate. Attention must shift to the manner in which *process* technologies change after the initial commercialization of the product.

It will be our contention in this section that the stabilization of process technology in the chemical industry is no less general a phenomenon than product standardization in the "systems-technology" industries described above.

The attention of R&D departments in the chemical industry is focused in two directions: first, in the search for new chemicals, drugs, plastics, and the development of associated commercial-scale production processes; second, in the search for improved production processes that will reduce the costs of producing well-known products (e.g., in the production of ethylene). Thus the effort to improve *products* is much less evident in the chemical industries than it is in, say, the computer, aircraft, and mechanical engineering industries (although the search for radically new products may be just as intense); the emphasis shifts to the improvement of *processes.*

It should be noted that since World War II chemical firms have increasingly employed plant contractors (Foster-Wheeler, Badger, Kellogg) to design and construct new plant, although the great majority of process innovations still originate within the chemical industry itself.[21] This division of labor has been well documented by Freeman (1968) in his study of the chemical process plant industry.

To return to the point of entry to the "cycle"—the development of a radically new product. The search for new chemical products is very expensive and risky, but the rewards to the successful innovator are very large. Chemical patents being generally difficult to circumvent, he can look forward to a considerable period of monopoly control in the world market, control that is strengthened by the innovator's early ability to benefit from scale economies. The timing and extent of production-transfer overseas will be decided by many factors internal and external to the industry: by the ease with which the chemical can be transported (some chemicals are so corrosive, or chemically unstable, that they cannot economically be traded over distances); by the success or failure of competitors in side-stepping the patent, either by developing a product with equivalent properties (e.g., IG Farben's development of Nylon-6) or by developing a different chemical route to the same product (the latter much more common)—in both cases reducing production costs; by the patent-holder's willingness to license production in other countries; by the level and spread of demand overseas; and by tariff and nontariff barriers, and the lure of cheap capital as discussed above.

After a certain time, the market "matures," and production is established in the major industrialized countries, either by successful imitation, or licensing, or direct investment. Comparative advantage in the production of, say, ethylene now depends almost entirely on production costs; demand is price-elastic.[22]

The product-cycle model predicts that by the time this phase is reached, production processes will normally be at an advanced stage of standardization. History suggests that this is very far from being the case. Striking advances have been made in process technology, usually to enable producers to reap greater and greater static economies of scale.

Acrylonitrile is perhaps the classic example. Originally manufactured (in the 1940s) by the dehydration of ethylene cyanohydrin, this process was superseded by one based on the addition of hydrogen cyanide to acetylene in the presence of cuprous chloride, which in turn was superseded in the 1960s by the Distillers/Sohio-Badger ammoxidation route. This last innovation reduced the U.K. price for acrylonitrile from £280 to £128 per ton and worldwide rendered plants based on earlier processes uneconomic.[23] From Stobaugh's data on plant licensing it is evident that Sohio was responsible for fourteen out of sixteen licenses granted throughout the Western world between 1960 and 1966.[24]

Monopoly control is as evident today as it was in the 1940s when acrylonitrile was first commercialized, and there are still no signs of process technologies stabilizing. The ammoxidation process is now being threatened by a process developed by Knapsack-Griesheim in Germany, in which lactonitrile (derived from reacting acetaldehyde with hydrogen cyanide) is dehydrated to acrylonitrile.

A similar progression has occurred in relation to many other intermediate chemicals—ammonia, phenol, methanol, and so on. Stone and Webster's recent development of the ultraselective cracking process for producing ethylene is another example of an innovation that has markedly reduced price and enlarged the output that can be attained from a single plant.

Comparative advantage thus lies firmly with manufacturers that are able to take advantage of these advances in process technology,[25] and to benefit from the increasing economies of scale that have usually attended (and stimulated) them. The size of the home market naturally has a strong influence on the ability of firms to compete internationally.

The move toward larger and larger plants has created a new set of problems. Plants must be run as near as possible to full capacity if they are to be economic; continuous supply must be maintained. Closing down a large plant usually results in considerable wastage, and extensive costs may be incurred by restarting (structural damage frequently occurs, and chemical deposits have to be removed). If the national market is unable to absorb the change in output following a new investment (capacity may suddenly be increased by as much as a third), the manufacturer will be forced to compete aggressively for overseas markets. The manufacturer also becomes more vulnerable to cyclical changes in demand.

The "stepwise" reductions in production costs that have characterized the industry since World War II have various important consequences for trading behavior and the location of production. First, a large home market is essential if scale economies are to be maximized; if a producer in a smaller market is to remain competitive, it will have to rely heavily on exports. Second, the oligopolistic structure of the industry will be threatened if price competition gets out of hand: hence the proliferation of cartels, long-term supply contracts with industries downstream, and antidumping agreements. Third, industries (or countries) lacking the very substantial capital resources required to keep abreast of the state-of-the-art, and lacking the base market to absorb the necessary supply levels, are unlikely to remain internationally competitive. This applies in particular to the less-developed economies. Fourth, imports from low factor cost locations to the developed countries may occur, but they will be temporary. The obsolescence rate in chemical plants is too rapid, and the costs of *sustaining* a comparative advantage too high. This is borne out by the virtual absence of "low-wage" trade in chemical products.[26] Fifth, industries in the advanced economies are under increasing pressure to stagger their investments in new plant in order to avoid oversupply and ruinous price wars.

Again, we are faced with a picture of competitive behavior at variance with the product-cycle theory: production processes rarely stabilize for any significant length of time, so that comparative advantage remains firmly with countries endowed with the capital, labor skills and market necessary for the *sustained* improvement of productive efficiency.[27]

PRODUCT-CYCLE "CONFORMISTS": CONSUMER ELECTRONICS

The consumer electronics industry is frequently referred to as conforming to the product-cycle description: innovation followed by gradual product and process standardization followed by a transfer of production to low-wage locations. The rapid build-up of U.S. imports of television sets and radios—products developed in their early days in the United States—is cited as evidence.

In looking at this industry, we are back once more to the question: why do some products standardize while others do not? Perhaps we need to answer a more basic question first: what do we mean by product standardization? Are we thinking in terms of the "performance characteristics" of the product (its outputs), or of the hardware from which it is constructed (whatever translates inputs into outputs)?

As has already been suggested, reasons for the standardization of outputs must be sought chiefly in the market. In the case of television sets, outputs have stabilized, on the one hand, because of operating standards agreed upon internationally by broadcasting authorities (frequencies, band widths, numbers of lines scanned), on the other hand because of the "ease" with which the qualitative aspects of consumer demand are satisfied. Once the average television set is capable of giving a steady, clear picture, demand becomes relatively inelastic to further performance increases (unless something radically new is on offer—e.g., the switch from black-and-white to color). Although product differentiation may still be important to the manufacturer, demand generally moves in the direction of high price elasticity.

Television assembly being highly labor-intensive, there are two possible routes open to the manufacturer to remain competitive; either he can minimize labor costs by transferring production to a low-wage location, or he can attempt to automate production (the relatively simple operation of "component insertion" constitutes around 75 percent of labor costs). Ironically, it has been the pace of technical change upstream in the electronic components industry that has given a clear advantage to low-wage production. Flexible production processes are essential if the manufacturer is to benefit from the new components that are continuously coming his way. The manufacturer who invests in an automated plant runs the risk of finding it obsolete before it is completed.

While the performance characteristics of both black-and-white and color television appear to have stabilized after an early period of uncertainty, the hardware has not. Again, we are faced with an example where the supply side is experiencing considerable technical change; production cannot be said to have standardized. Now that both Japanese and American industries are investing large sums in developing automated production lines in which component insertion is computer-guided (so that product change can be achieved by reprogramming), now that component miniaturization has greatly reduced the number of components typically to be found in a television set, it is conceivable that TV production will become highly capital-intensive in the future, and comparative advantage will once again return to the capital-abundant countries.[28]

The dominant unsettling influence of components industries upstream has characterized consumer electronics production (and electronic capital goods production, for that matter) since World War II. Again we are faced with industrial behavior that does not neatly fit the product-cycle description. On the surface, products appear relatively stable, as do factor-intensities of production. But product stability, where it has occurred, has been "imposed" on producers by international regulations and an undemanding public. And production has remained labor-intensive as a result of technological *instability,* not stability.

CONCLUDING COMMENTS ON THE NEO-TECHNOLOGY THEORIES

While the above descriptions are highly simplified and contain many points of substance that may be open to challenge, they serve to illustrate some of the shortcomings of the product-cycle theory. Here we very briefly summarise the most important points, and, again very briefly, discuss implications for the empirical part of the paper.

(a) The neoclassical model predicts that, given factor-intensities of production associated with particular techniques, production will be located in different countries according to their relative factor endowments. The product-cycle theory extends this factor-endowment explanation by adding entrepreneurial and technical skills to the list of endowments; and by proposing that as products develop and "mature," production moves crabwise across countries, "seeking out" locations with appropriate factor proportions. After the initial perturbation, there is a return to neoclassical orthodoxy.

As we have tried to demonstrate, technical stability—or the tendency toward it—was the exception, not the rule, in the historical period in question. Industries and countries were exposed to, and participated in, what Schumpeter termed the "perennial gale of creative destruction." Under such conditions, innovative efforts pre-empt the "natural" tendency of production to be reallocated in accordance with neoclassical and product-cycle predictions.

In these circumstances, factor mobility is best regarded as a response by firms to a variety of politico-economic situations and opportunities, at home and abroad: tariff and nontariff barriers, cheap factors of production, and so on. It is not the result of an inexorable stabilization of production techniques after first discovery.

(b) In the knowledge-creating industries, innovation is a necessary but not sufficient condition for competitive success. The extent to which a firm can *sustain* its position in world markets depends not only on its creative abilities (which include the abilities to absorb new ideas and techniques), but also on the productive resources at its disposal, and on the efficiency with which it operates them. In circumstances where factor mobility is condoned and even encouraged, these resources may lie both inside and outside the parent country.

These resources include capital, land, and labor, in both the neoclassical and Johnsonian definitions of the term. They should not, however, be regarded as in any way fixed or ahistorical. They are constantly being transformed, qualitatively and quantitatively, by technical change. The economists' three factors of production also fail to capture the benefits accruing to the producer from being a part of a developed industrial economy. In many respects the surrounding infrastructure acts as an "endowment" to the manufacturer; just as a nearby source of wood pulp confers a comparative advantage to the paper manufacturer, so a nearby source of specialist jigs and tools confers a competitive advantage to the manufacturer of textile machinery. The importance of these "external economies" tends to be underestimated by economists.

(c) The product-cycle theorists erred in their attempts to build a general model of product behaviour that could encompass all research-intensive industries. If this was not their intention, they failed to define the boundaries between applicability and inapplicability. It is clear from the above that fundamental differences exist between product groups. To what level of disaggregation one has to descend before generalizations can be made is an important question. Does the development of manufacture in organic chemicals resemble that in inorganic chemicals? Can the chemical industry be said to be roughly homogeneous in its product behavior? New categorizations of industrial behavior are badly needed, going beyond the economists' factor-intensity breakdowns to include such qualitative aspects as the nature of market demand, infrastructural dependence, and competitive pressures.

(d) To quote Gruber, Mehta and Vernon (1967), "All roads lead to a link between export performance and R&D." If the interpretation in this section is correct, one would expect the *dynamic* effect of industrial innovation on the location of comparative advantage and market power to be discernible in trends in postwar export trade. Within the "innovation-intensive" industries where (we suggest) innovation has been a necessary, but not sufficient, condition for the accumulation of capital and the growth of output (and exports), one would expect the technological leader to have strengthened his position in world markets at the expense of the technological laggard. There should be some correlation between relative innovative efforts and movements in trade shares.

These ideas will be followed up in Chapter IV. Two final points should be kept in mind. First, there are contexts in which export performance may not be a good proxy for comparative advantage. Foreign investment may increase or decrease apparent comparative advantage, depending on whether it leads to export supplementation or replacement. Secondly, we are not implying that innovative effort is exogeneous to the economic system. Demand for labor-saving devices within the home economy, competitive pressures, cash flow, and expectations of economic growth at home and abroad may all influence the extent to which firms divert resources into product and process development. This carries with it the implication that trading performance influences innovative effort, just as innovative effort influences trading performances: the two variables may be mutually reinforcing.

This brings us to an important qualification to the argument in the above pages, namely, that it is built around the observation of Western capitalism in an historical period—1945–1973—during which technical change proceeded at an unprecedented rate, cause and effect of unusually rapid economic growth and liberal trading. It appears that we are now entering an era of less peaceful economic relationships, one in which technical change may have a qualitatively different influence on trading patterns. Great care must therefore be taken in extrapolating the argument to present and future economic conditions.

Notes

1. As the most coherent exponent of the product-cycle theory, Vernon will be cited as its author in the following pages. This is not to deny Hirsch's and other authors' important contributions.

2. In his 1966 paper, Vernon understated the stimulus that oligopolistic competition gives to the development of new products and processes. As will become apparent, this is a serious deficiency in his original model. He has since made amends [Vernon (1973)], without fully recognizing the embarrassment it causes to the product-cycle theory—at least when innovations arise from within an established oligopolistic industrial structure.

3. Vernon stresses that his explanation relates only to labor-saving innovations.

4. This section draws heavily on Rothwell's (1976a) study of innovation in the European textile machinery industry.

5. It is important to realize that sophistication may imply a reduction in complexity. As in most branches of engineering, there is a constant struggle to increase performance without being overwhelmed (technologically and economically) by complexity: the search for simplicity is an integral part of technological development. Hence the engineer's partiality to "elegant" solutions.

6. A good (although extreme) example is the recent development of open-end spinning. The technique was pioneered by the Czech textile-machinery industry, the first version allowing rotor speeds of up to 40,000 rpm. Western European producers reacted by introducing machines capable of an upper limit of 60,000 rpm, but the Czechs have subsequently pushed rotor speeds up to 90,000 rpm, as well as improving the quality and reliability of the original machine. Rotor speeds are, of course, only a proxy for total machine capability. In 1976, the Czechs contributed 70 percent of the world's exports of open-ended spinning machinery.

7. Production of textile machinery has remained concentrated in a few OECD countries (especially the United States, the United Kingdom, Germany, and Switzerland). It is especially interesting that Switzerland has become a major supplier, despite an unimportant domestic market. This suggests that strong demand in nearby markets (Italy, France, Germany) can act as a "domestic" market to an internationally minded, multilingual industry.

8. This does not necessarily mean that production of earlier generations of equipment will cease. The older machines may offer textile industries in some countries greater savings in operating costs (plus social benefits such as employment preservation) than the new, more capital-intensive machine. See Shepherd (1974). However, Cooper (1974) found in the jute industry that demand for earlier generations of equipment tended to fall off fairly rapidly, even in countries that might be expected (neoclassically) to benefit from their use. It is important to realize that successive generations of machines not only offer savings in production costs, but extend the range and quality of manufactured output. This is especially true in metalworking production. The modern milling machine is able to achieve an accuracy and quality of finish beyond the capabilities of earlier generations. As such, stringent market requirements frequently militate against investment in older vintages, overruling calculations based on consideration of factor costs.

9. New machine tools and instrumentation also importantly extend the range of production possibilities.

10. The skill-content of this supply has changed over time, both in design and

production. Designing textile machinery is no longer the task of mechanical engineers alone.

11. In this respect, it is important to remember that as with other engineering goods, textile machinery is "multifaceted"—it proceeds along several technological dimensions concurrently. A machine is an amalgamation of, say, lubrication channels, electric motors, transmissions, bearings, vibration dampers. . . , far removed from the homogeneous commodities favored by neoclassical economists. This plurality naturally increases the potential for product improvement, as well as increasing the vulnerability of the manufacturer that fails to take full advantage of external advances in the state of the art.

12. Much of the confusion in the product-cycle literature arises from the tendency to associate "standards" with "standardization." It is of course true that technical standards play an important part in industrial life, by cutting production costs, insuring compatibility with other manufacturers' equipment (standard interfaces), by allowing supply industries to exact economies of scale, and so on. It should, however, be clearly understood that the development of technical standards following the birth of a new industry or technology does *not* entail the stabilization (or standardization) of the product. As any design engineer will attest, standards if anything *ease* the task of product development.

13. Rothwell (1976b).

14. The contribution of product (as against process) innovation to reductions in production costs has received too little attention in the literature.

15. See especially Surrey and Chesshire (1970) on the heavy electrical industry; Sawers and Miller (1967) on the aircraft industry; Harman (1971) on the computer industry; Freeman (1955) on electronic capital goods; and the various journals serving the different product groups (e.g., *American Machinist* in relation to metalworking machine tools).

16. The largest European manufacturer of mining equipment, Westphalia Lunen, started manufacturing shearer-loaders in 1971. This was part of their strategy to develop their technological expertise to the extent that they were able to market a complete coal-mining system—an integrated range of products. The industry is moving towards a situation where it is no longer product v. product competition, but mining system v. mining system.

17. The underground coal-mining machinery industry is unusual in that many of the inventions have originated in the UK National Coal Board (NCB), which has powerful central laboratories, and have subsequently been licensed to the manufacturers. This explains the unusually short "imitation"-lag evident in some cases (e.g., the bi-directional shearer-loader). Where a manufacturer has been responsible for an innovation (e.g., Eickhoff and the thin-seam shearer-loader), the manufacturers have had more difficulty in finding an effective response.

Two other points: first, the number of machines introduced per annum appear to have declined after 1965. As the patent statistics show, this has not been accompanied by a slackening of innovative activity. Much of the effort has been directed at improving "established" machines. The bi-directional shearer-loader marketed in 1976 is a very different animal from that first introduced in 1962. Improvements include the attachment of dozer plates, nucleonic sensing devices, powered cowl, rack-and-pinion haulage, pick-face flushing, load shields, and so on. Second, as many of the innovations listed in Figure 3 have failed commercially as have succeeded. Manufacturers are operating in conditions of high uncertainty as to the path market demand will follow in the future.

18. Sciberras (1976) in his study of the semiconductor industry found that the determination to maximize profits and to prevent market entry by foreign producers frequently led to multinationals' investing in production facilities overseas when their monopoly control over national and international markets was as yet uncontested.

19. One would expect capital movements between the most advanced industrial nations to be less affected by infrastructural problems (i.e., the absence of a network of experienced suppliers) than capital movements between developed and underdeveloped nations. Of course, it is not uncommon for firms to bypass nontariff barriers by setting up a part of their production process in the protected country (usually the least skill- and capital-intensive part), importing the rest of the product from the parent country. It should be remembered that "subsystems" of an advanced technology product may have very different factor-intensities of production, so that production can be split up and located to give maximum penetration of world markets, and to optimize the return to the producer. Spreading manufacture internationally can also lower political barriers to trade.

20. We are here concerned with intermediate chemicals. In other areas of the industry (e.g., fine chemicals), products tend to be less stable. The point of concentrating on intermediates is to illustrate that even if products are relatively stable, process instability may contradict the product-cycle (and technology-gap) descriptions.

21. The division of labor between chemical companies and plant contractors is seldom clear-cut, as it frequently involves close collaboration from early innovation to final construction. For instance, Kellogg worked closely with ICI on the development of the naphtha-cracking process for the production of ethylene.

22. Since demand for chemicals is generally sensitive to price levels, tariff barriers provide greater protection than they do for the products described in the section on "Product-cycle 'Nonconformists.'"

23. See Rueben and Burstall (1973).

24. See Stobaugh (1968). Stobaugh's study of the petrochemical industry is

widely regarded as supporting the product-cycle theory. It is open to criticism on three grounds. First, the sample is limited in size (nine intermediate petrochemical products), and the data relating to it is variable in quality. For instance, stages of the product-cycle inhabited historically by Isoprene and Orthoxylene are inferred from US consumption data for the yars 1963–65 (Isoprene), 1960 and 1965–66 (Orthoxylene). Second, the theoretical justification for using historic growth rates of consumption to delineate the stages of the cycle is unclear (the techniques used to assess these growth rates are also questionable, especially in the light of the imperfect data-base). Third, the study provides an insufficient test of the technological aspects of the product-cycle theory—there is no technological evidence that established empirically that processes have standardized as the product has "aged," thereby lowering entry barriers. Indeed, some of Stobaugh's data (e.g. in relation to acrylonitrile and methanol) appears consistent with an altogether more unsettled and stochastic pattern of process development.

25. The significance of improvements to processes already operating is stressed by Mann (1968): "The useful life of a process can be prolonged by a continuous technical effort to devise both major and minor improvements, which could, for example, result in greater throughput, savings in utilities, more efficient utilisation of raw materials and better products quality. Later plants and extensions can be designed to take full advantage of the experience gained in the first unit. Thus the intrinsic value of a process will increase over a period of years and it may in this way be able to compete successfully with younger processes which have advantages in the long-term." The shift of comparative advantage from operators of old plants to operators of new plants may thus be a more gradual process than might otherwise be expected. Schott and Müller (1975) also emphasize the importance of process improvement.

26. This applies in particular to trade in intermediates (ethylene, ammonia, etc.). Where the fabrication of final products is rather more labor-intensive, and less sensitive to economies of scale, low-wage countries may be in a stronger competitive position.

27. This certainly applied before the mid-1970s, but there is growing talk in the chemical industry of an upper limit in scale economies being reached. With individual plants supplying larger and larger chunks of national demand, the commercial risks of expanding plant size are growing. The determinants of comparative advantage may be changing, and one can envisage a situation in which governments will be increasingly drawn into protecting home markets.

28. This has in fact happened in the production of electronic calculators. The advent of LSI components has translated a labor-intensive industry into a capital-intensive industry in a very short space of time.

Chapter III

International Trading Patterns

In Chapter IV we shall return to links between innovation and trading performance. The analysis will be focused on OECD trade in manufactured goods. Here we wish to examine trading developments within and without the OECD, and to include primary products in our list of commodities; we shall restrict ourselves mainly to empirical observations. As previously, the discussion will be centered on the historical period 1945–1973.

THE GROWTH OF WORLD TRADE

A remarkable feature of the postwar period up to 1973 was the unprecedentedly rapid expansion of international trade. For the first time in modern history the volume and value of world trade increased at a greater rate than industrial production.[1] In other words, an increasing proportion of the output of the average Western economy was traded in the international marketplace. This trend can be seen clearly in Table 1 (the United Kingdom and Denmark being the only exceptions) which also illustrates the extent to which countries differ in the proportion of their national products traded internationally.

This variation between regions in the rates of growth of trade in relation to production can be further seen in Table 2. With regard to Japan and the EEC, exports and production grew rapidly throughout the 1960s, exports outstripping production; whereas in the United States and the United Kingdom exports only began to outgrow production in

Table 1

Foreign trade[a] as Percentage of GDP

	1955	1971
Austria	19.1	22.0
Belgium-Luxembourg	30.9	44.3
Denmark	26.7	25.1[b]
Finland	18.1	22.7
France	9.9	13.0
Germany (Federal Republic)	13.8	16.9
Greece	11.9	16.2[b]
Ireland	30.5	35.5
Italy	9.5	15.4
Netherlands	37.6	40.1
Norway	25.4	25.6
Portugal	18.4	20.7
Spain	7[c]	11.0[b]
Sweden	20.5	20.5
Switzerland	22.3	27.0
Turkey	5.4	5.7[b]
United Kingdom	18.3	17.1
Yugoslavia	–	18.2[b]
United States	3.6	4.5
Japan	9.4	9.6

[a] Average of imports and exports (f.o.b.) of merchandise. The countries for which the import ratio normally exceeds the export ratio by more than about 4 percent of GDP on an f.o.b. basis are: Austria, Greece, Ireland, Norway, Portugal, Spain, Yugoslavia. Only in West Germany has there been a persistant export surplus (on an f.o.b. basis) equal to around 4 percent of GDP (largely offset by a regular deficit on invisible account).

[b] 1970.

[c] 1960.

Source: IMF/TBRD: International Financial Statistics Supplement, December 1972. Reproduced from Saunders (1975), p. 91.

the latter half of the decade. Similarly, comparison of export and production growth in less-developed countries shows wide divergence (e.g., between Taiwan and India), although the overall trend was for growth to be slower than in the OECD, and for rates of increase in trade to be

Table 2

Industrial Production and Export Trends
(constant factor costs)

Year	World Prod.	World Exp.	U.S. Prod.	U.S. Exp.	Japan Prod.	Japan Exp.	EEC 6 Prod.	EEC 6 Exp.	U.K. Prod.	U.K. Exp.
1961	88	87	89	90	84	78	90	86	96	95
1963	100	100	100	100	100	100	100	100	100	100
1965	114	122	115	118	120	155	111	127	112	108
1967	128	140	131	137	162	192	119	149	113	111
1969	148	180	145	166	222	294	143	202	123	140
1971	153	231	139	192	270	441	156	271	126	153

Source: National Institute Economic Review, No. 63, Feb. 1973.

rather more convergent with rates of increase in production. Within and without the OECD, it is apparent that countries benefited unequally from, and contributed unequally to, the general expansion of international trade. A substantial "reallocation" of economic power was taking place.

GEOGRAPHICAL CONCENTRATION OF TRADE

During the 1930s, bilateral trade predominated, as countries sought to preserve employment and the credibility of their currencies. Goods continued to flow across boundaries, but the relatively free competition that had prevailed before 1929 was undermined by restrictive regulations and bilateral agreements. Germany traded with the Balkan states, France and Britain with their respective empires, and the United States withdrew into isolationism.

Multilateral trading returned in the wake of the postwar economic recovery. Under American financial and political pressure, exchange rates were stabilized, and the various obstacles to multilateral trading within the OECD were progressively (if not completely) removed.

The ensuing expansion of world trade has already been noted. But no less striking a feature of the 1950s and 1960s was the growing intensification of trade *within* the Western industrial bloc. In 1962, trade between

OECD member countries represented close to two-thirds of their total world trade (65.3 percent of exports, 65.8 percent imports). By 1972, this proportion had increased to three-quarters (74.9 percent of imports and exports—Table 3). A remarkable shift in the distribution of world trade was occurring throughout this period, caused partly by changes in the physical volume and composition of trade, partly by changes of the relative prices of primary and manufactured products. As a consequence the less-developed countries experienced a gradual deterioration in their terms of trade (a typical unit of an exportable commodity was yielding a decreasing volume of imports).

What was the geographical pattern of trade within the OECD, and how was it changing?

In 1972, the United States, Japan, and Canada accounted for 30.3 percent, OECD Europe 68 percent, of intra-OECD exports (Table 4).[2] OECD Europe thus occupied a dominating position in OECD trade, and, for that matter, in world trade. Furthermore, 85 percent of OECD Europe's exports remained within European boundaries.

As Chesney and Cooper (1970) have pointed out, an intensification of trading relations took place in the 1950s and 1960s within two geographical segments of the OECD, while exchanges between the two segments increased only slightly (in relation to total OECD trade). On the

Table 3

Intra - OECD Exports and Imports as a Proportion of Total OECD Trade (1962 - 1972)

$ billion

	OECD Exports A	Intra-OECD Exports B	B/A %	OECD Imports C	Intra-OECD Exports D	D/C %
1962	88.4	57.7	65.3	91.9	60.5	65.8
1964	109.0	73.0	67.8	113.3	76.5	67.5
1966	132.7	91.8	69.1	138.5	95.9	69.2
1968	159.7	113.6	71.1	166.2	116.4	71.2
1970	214.7	155.7	72.5	220.9	160.9	72.8
1972	290.1	217.3	74.9	297.9	223.2	74.9

Source: OECD, Trade by Commodities, Series B.

Table 4

Shares in Intra-OECD Trade, 1972 (by value)

	US	Canada	Japan	OECD-Europe	(of which intra-Europe)	Other	Total
Exports	14.8	8.3	7.2	67.9	(58.0)	1.8	100.0
Imports	17.9	7.6	5.3	67.5	(56.2)	1.7	100.0

Source: OECD, Trade by Commodities, Series B.

one hand, U.S. trade shifted in favor of closer links with Japan and Canada, mostly at the expense of exchanges with the underdeveloped countries. Between 1963 and 1972, U.S. exports to Canada and Japan increased from 25 percent to 35 percent of total U.S. exports (Table 5).[3]

On the other hand, trade within Europe intensified, although it is notable that trading between the two European Customs Unions—the EEC and EFTA—only began to pull out of a relative decline toward the end of the 1960s. Thus, intra-EEC exports rose from 42.4 percent to 49.8 percent of total EEC exports between 1963 and 1972, while the share of exports to EFTA fell from 22.0 percent to 17.8 percent (Table 6). Similarly, intra-EFTA exports rose from 22.7 percent to 29.0 percent of total

Table 5

U.S. Destination of Exports, 1963 - 1972 (by value)

							Percentages
Year	World	Developed* world	EEC	EFTA	Canada	Japan	Less developed world
1963	100	58.0	17.0	11.0	17.7	7.3	42.0
1966	100	64.3	17.6	10.4	21.7	7.7	35.7
1969	100	70.0	18.4	10.4	23.9	9.2	30.0
1972	100	69.0	17.8	9.3	24.8	10.0	31.0

Source: UN, Yearbook of International Trade Statistics, 1972.
* Includes Eastern bloc

Table 6

EEC Destination of Exports, 1963 - 1972 (by value)

Percentages

Year	World	Developed world	EEC	EFTA	UK	Canada Japan U.S.	Less developed world
1963	100	79.2	42.4	22.0	5.3	8.9	20.8
1966	100	80.5	44.1	19.9	4.8	9.6	19.5
1969	100	82.2	48.2	17.5	4.4	9.8	17.8
1972	100	83.2	49.8	17.8	5.1	9.2	16.8

Source: UN, Yearbook of International Trade Statistics, 1972.

Table 7

EFTA: Destination of Exports, 1963 - 1972 (by value)

Percentages

Year	World	Developed world	EEC	EFTA	Canada Japan U.S.	U.K.	Less developed world
1963	100	75.3	27.7	22.7	11.4	6.7	24.3
1966	100	79.4	25.4	25.2	13.9	7.1	20.6
1969	100	77.8	25.3	26.6	13.6	7.2	22.2
1972	100	79.6	26.0	29.0	13.4	7.9	20.4

Source: UN, Yearbook of International Trade Statistics, 1972.

Table 8

Shares of Manufactured Export Trade of Ten Major OECD Countries

Percentages

	U.S.	Canada	Japan	Sweden	U.K.	EEC-6	TOTAL
1963-1965	22.2	5.7	8.3	3.7	14.0	46.2	100.0
1971-1973	17.2	6.4	12.6	3.7	9.8	50.4	100.0

Source: OECD, Trade by Commodities, Series B.

EFTA exports over the same period, while the share of exports to the EEC declined from 27.7 percent to 26.0 percent (Table 7).

Accompanying these changes was a marked shift in the trading "power" of the major OECD countries. As is apparent in Table 8, the EEC and Japan increased their shares of manufactured export trade at the expense of the United States and the United Kingdom.

THE PRODUCT CONCENTRATION OF TRADE

Parallel and related to geographical concentration was the increasing dominance of certain types of commodity in international trade (Table 9). Over the period 1962–1972, the proportion of intra-OECD trade comprising the main SITC manufactured product groups—chemicals (5), manufactured goods classified by materials (6), machinery and transport equipment (7), other manufactures (8)—rose from 66.9 percent to 75.5 percent, the dramatically increasing share of "machinery and transport equipment" (27.6 percent to 35.4 percent) in intra-OECD trade outweighing the declining share of "manufactured goods classified by materials" (23.9 percent to 21.6 percent).[4] It is also apparent in Table 9 that the growth of export trade accelerated in the latter half of the decade, as did the value of trade in primary products—symptomatic of the chronic imbalances between supply and demand that emerged in the early 1970s, and that in large part led to our present economic difficulties.

The combined effects of geographical and product concentration can be seen in Table 10, which shows the concentration of OECD intra-trade by each product group, in relation to total OECD trade. In every product group, primary and manufactured, export trade within the OECD bloc increased relative to total OECD trade; a diminishing fraction of trade was finding its way to the less-developed countries, especially in the SITC manufacturing sections 5–8. Moreover, the import statistics reveal that the OECD countries were approaching self-sufficiency in the production of manufactured goods.

Product concentration may be further illustrated by examining the changing structure of United Kingdom imports and exports between 1951 and 1972 (Table 11). With regard to imports, trade in primary products declined in economic significance, while imports of manufactured goods rose substantially. With regard to exports, the principal

Table 9

Intra-OECD Exports by Main SITC Product-Groups 1962 - 1972*

Year	Product Group	0	1	2	3	4	5	6	7	8
		Percentage Share of Each Product Group in Total								
1962	100	12.2	2.1	11.3	5.2	0.6	7.2	23.9	27.6	8.2
1964	100	11.6	2.1	11.4	4.6	0.6	7.7	24.2	28.0	8.7
1966	100	10.9	1.9	9.9	3.8	0.4	7.7	24.0	30.5	9.4
1968	100	9.3	1.8	9.5	3.8	0.4	8.2	23.5	32.8	9.7
1970	100	8.9	1.6	8.7	4.0	0.5	8.1	22.2	34.2	9.9
1972	100	9.5	1.7	8.0	4.0	0.4	8.0	21.7	35.4	10.4
		Indices of the Value of Trade								
								1962 = 100, 1968 =100		
1962	100	100	100	100	100	100	100	100	100	100
1964	126	118	121	126	111	118	132	128	128	135
1966	159	142	143	139	118	118	169	159	175	181
1968	100	100	100	100	100	100	100	100	100	100
1970	137	130	117	126	142	174	136	135	143	140
1972	191	194	174	162	202	200	187	176	206	205

* Standard International Trade Classification (SITC):

0 = Food and live animals
1 = Beverages and tobacco
2 = Crude materials
3 = Mineral fuels
4 = Animal and vegetable oils
5 = Chemicals
6 = Manufactured goods classified by materials
7 = Machinery and transport equipment
8 = Other manufactures
9 = Unclassified

Source: OECD, Trade by Commodities, Series B.

changes occurred within the manufacturing sector: the "innovation-intensive" manufacturing industries—chemicals, machinery and transport equipment, other industries (which includes instruments)—increased their shares of total UK exports; while the more "traditional" manufacturing industries—textiles, rubber, paper and printing—have steadily declined in economic importance.

Table 10

OECD Intra-Trade as Percentage of Total OECD Trade in SITC Product Groups, 1962 - 1972 (by value)*

Percentages

	Year	0	1	2	3	4	5	6	7	8
					Product group					
	1962	46.8	67.8	46.0	28.5	49.7	91.0	81.5	97.6	88.4
Imports	1966	50.0	79.0	47.7	26.3	46.0	90.5	78.5	98.0	87.8
	1969	50.7	81.9	51.5	25.8	47.3	91.5	79.6	97.6	85.6
	1972	58.1	86.4	62.0	26.4	50.8	92.3	81.7	96.3	81.6
	1962	70.8	74.0	82.8	81.3	61.0	58.6	66.8	56.7	68.9
Exports	1966	70.0	86.6	84.9	82.7	59.6	60.8	71.8	63.5	76.7
	1969	75.6	77.8	86.2	88.6	63.0	65.8	73.6	67.0	79.4
	1972	74.9	81.4	84.9	87.5	61.2	68.5	75.9	71.6	83.6

* SITC Product-groups as per Table 9.
Source: OECD, Trade by Commodities, Series B.

This latter point brings out another important long-term development: the movement in the commodity pattern of trade in manufactures from, in particular, textiles to chemicals and engineering goods (this trend has been apparent for at least a century). Thus, in 1929, machinery, transport equipment, and chemicals accounted for 32.8 percent of the twelve main exporting nations' manufactured exports, while textiles accounted for 28.7 percent (Table 12). By 1959, respective shares had shifted to 53.3 percent and 11.1 percent.[5] Measured in terms of weight, the trend was even more remarkable (Table 13). The effect is blunted when trade is measured by current value as technological change has resulted in sharp falls in the real value per ton of output.

Table 11

U.K.: Structure of Total Trade Flows by SITC Product Groups, 1951 – 1972*
(by value)

Percentages

Product groups	Exports 1951	Exports 1967	Exports 1972	Imports 1951	Imports 1967	Imports 1972
0	3.7	3.3	3.5	30.3	18.6	15.2
1	2.4	3.2	3.2	2.8	1.8	1.2
2	4.0	2.9	3.2	36.1	20.5	16.1
3	2.7	2.6	2.4	8.1	17.7	19.8
4	0.2	0.1	0.1	2.8	1.4	1.1
5	7.7	9.8	9.9	2.9	5.0	5.3
6	35.8	25.0	24.1	13.4	15.6	16.4
7	34.5	42.0	41.2	2.1	12.9	16.5
8	7.0	8.2	9.5	1.0	4.5	7.1
9	2.0	2.8	2.8	0.4	2.0	1.4

* SITC product groups as per Table 9.
Source: OECD, Trade by Commodities, Series B.

Table 12

Commodity Pattern of Trade in Manufacturers, 1929 – 1959: Exports from 12 Main Exporting Countries (by value)

Percentages

	1929	1937	1950	1955	1959
Metals	11.9	15.3	12.9	15.0	13.5
Machinery	14.5	16.0	20.7	22.3	24.8
Transport equipment	9.8	10.5	14.2	15.3	16.5
Other metal goods	5.9	6.5	4.9	4.8	4.2
Chemicals	8.5	10.6	10.5	11.4	12.0
Textiles and clothing	28.7	21.5	19.9	13.4	11.1
Other manufacturers	21.0	19.5	17.0	17.9	17.9
TOTAL	100	100	100	100	100

Source: Maizels (1971), p. 163.

Table 13

Commodity Pattern of Trade in Manufacturers, 1929 - 1959: Exports from 12 Main Exporting Countries (by weight)

	Index numbers, 1929 = 100				
	1929	1937	1950	1955	1959
Metals	100	88	98	136	164
Machinery	100	78	132	188	238
Transport equipment	100	87	151	214	282
Other metal goods	100	72	78	94	96
Chemicals	100	93	142	242	356
Textiles and clothing	100	84	74	81	94
Other manufacturers	100	84	93	137	174
TOTAL	100	83	104	144	182

Source: Maizels (1971), p. 165.

PRODUCT SPECIALIZATION WITHIN THE OECD

As one would expect, considerable variation exists between OECD countries as regards the product structure of their intra-OECD imports and exports (Table 14). For instance, the United States is less dependent on imports of food and raw materials than is the United Kingdom; and Canada relies less on exports of manufactured goods than does Japan.

It is clear from Table 14 that EEC import and export structures come closest to the OECD average. This is hardly surprising, as the EEC accounts for over 50 percent of OECD trade and therefore plays a large hand in determining its "shape." Rather than comparing patterns of trade from country to country, it is more instructive to consider the degree to which each region's import and export structures are "matched." This may be done by calculating the ratios of exports to imports within each product group (Table 15).

Leaving aside the insignificant SITC section 4 (animal and vegetable oils), it is evident that EEC export and import *structures* are most closely matched (ratios ranging from 0.44 to 1.26 in 1972).[6] The United Kingdom and the United States export and import patterns are less equiva-

Table 14

Structure of Intra-OECD Imports and Exports by SITC Product Group
1965 - 1972*

	Area	Year	0	1	2	3	4	5	6	7	8	Total
Imports	OECD	1965	11.9	1.8	11.0	4.1	0.6	7.8	23.9	27.3	9.8	100.0
		1971	8.8	1.6	7.6	4.0	0.5	8.1	22.2	36.0	10.2	100.0
	EEC	1967	12.5	1.5	10.9	4.0	0.6	8.9	24.2	26.2	9.1	100.0
		1972	12.2	1.5	8.6	3.5	0.5	9.2	23.4	29.0	10.7	100.0
	USA	1965	5.8	3.8	12.0	3.1	0.2	4.4	32.4	21.6	11.9	100.0
		1972	5.5	2.3	6.6	4.4	0.1	4.3	22.4	40.1	11.4	100.0
	UK	1967	20.7	3.2	12.0	5.1	0.7	7.4	20.9	21.1	7.3	100.0
		1972	16.7	2.9	9.8	3.9	0.5	7.6	19.7	28.7	9.2	100.0
Exports	OECD	1965	11.7	1.9	10.4	4.2	0.6	7.7	24.5	28.9	9.0	100.0
		1971	9.5	1.7	8.0	4.0	0.4	8.0	21.7	35.4	10.4	100.0
	EEC	1967	9.3	1.3	5.2	4.5	0.4	9.6	26.2	31.5	10.9	100.0
		1972	9.6	1.5	3.8	4.4	0.4	9.9	23.8	34.1	11.7	100.0
	USA	1965	14.9	2.2	13.8	4.4	1.2	8.8	12.0	35.5	6.6	100.0
		1972	9.5	2.0	12.2	4.0	0.5	7.9	10.4	44.5	7.2	100.0
	UK	1967	3.9	3.8	3.6	3.7	0.1	8.6	26.9	37.6	9.1	100.0
		1972	4.0	3.5	3.9	3.3	0.1	9.0	26.3	38.5	10.3	100.0

* SITC product groups as per Table 9.
Source: OECD, Trade by Commodities, Series B.

lent (ratios ranging from 0.24 to 1.34 for the United Kingdom, 0.46 to 1.85 for the United States). It should be also noted that EEC (and to a lesser extent the United Kingdom) imports and exports were most nearly matched in manufactured goods (sections 5–8).

Another important trend in OECD trading is discernible in Table 15. Although it has only been possible to make the calculations for a six-year period (eight-year for the United States), the figures suggest that, with the exception of sections 2 and 3 (where some divergence would be expected), the product structures of imports and exports were converging

Table 15

Percent Intra-OECD Exports / Percent Intra-OECD Imports by SITC product group*

		0	1	2	3	4	5	6	7	8	Total
EEC	1967	0.74	0.87	0.48	1.12	0.67	1.08	1.08	1.20	1.20	1.00
	1972	0.79	1.00	0.44	1.26	0.80	1.08	1.02	1.18	1.09	1.00
USA	1965	2.57	0.58	1.15	1.42	6.00	2.00	0.37	1.64	0.55	1.00
	1972	1.73	0.87	1.85	0.91	5.00	1.84	0.46	1.11	0.63	1.00
UK	1967	0.19	1.19	0.30	0.73	0.14	1.16	1.29	1.78	1.25	1.00
	1972	0.24	1.21	0.40	0.85	0.20	1.18	1.33	1.34	1.12	1.00

* SITC product group as per Table 9.
Source: Table 14.

in each of the regions. Again, the trend was most marked in product groups 5–8.

These observations point to growing structural similarities between the trading patterns of OECD member countries, in particular within Western Europe. Although one would hardly expect this to be accompanied by an equally rapid convergence in output and employment patterns, movement in this direction has been remarked upon by various authors [e.g., Saunders (1975)]. The implications are twofold: first, that there has been a growing division of labor, or specialization, *within* product groups in the OECD; second, that manufacturing industries have been involved in a growing interchange of goods—industrial production has become more tightly intermeshed across international boundaries, in part due to the trading activities of multinational companies.

A glance at the disaggregated Trade Statistics (OECD Trade by Commodities, series C) suggests that specialization within the OECD goes very deep, and that goods are exchanged internationally within product groups even at the highest observable levels of disaggregation. To give an example, each of the major OECD countries—the United States, Japan, Canada, OECD Europe—acts as both the source and destination of substantial amounts of goods belonging to the SITC product-group 861.97 (instruments for measuring or controlling of liquids); in 1972 the United States exported $2.3 million worth of such goods to Germany, and imported $2 million worth from Germany.

In the light of our discussion in previous sections, the ubiquity of product specialization within the OECD comes as little surprise. It is the result, on the one hand, of rising (and to some extent converging) income levels and increasingly diversified patterns of demand; and on the other hand, of industrial efforts to gain (and circumvent) monopoly control via innovation and product differentiation.[7]

"R&D-INTENSITY" OF OECD TRADE

The structure of OECD trade can be looked at from a rather different viewpoint by examining the "relative R&D intensity" of the exports of the major trading nations; that is, examining the extent to which patterns of specialization are correlated, from country to country, with the R&D intensity of production in different product groups.[8] We would expect a strong correlation for the United States (specialization in the exports of aircraft, computers, machine tools, etc.); a relatively weak correlation for Canada (specialization in exports of automobiles, food, paper, and wood). We can also look at the directions in which these relative patterns were moving in the 1960s by performing two sets of correlations—one for 1963-1965, the other for 1971-1973.[9] Tables 16 and 17 set out the ten major OECD exporters' shares of total exports for each product group, in a 17-product-group breakdown of manufactured goods for the two periods.[10] In Tables 18 and 19, these shares are "normalized" by each country's share in the export of total manufactured goods, to give a measure of relative specialization. Thus, if the normalized export share of country A in commodity B is greater than unity, it indicates that country A specializes in the export of commodity B relative to country A's exports of other manufactured goods *and* to the exports of the remaining nine countries in commodity B (e.g., the United Kingdom specializes in the export of mechanical machinery and drugs). If the normalized export share is less than unity, country A is relatively weak in the export of commodity B (e.g., the United Kingdom in wood and ships). Normalized export shares are frequently used as proxies for comparative advantage.

If the product groups listed in Tables 16–19 are ranked according to R&D intensity, rank correlations with normalized export shares give us a condensed view of the structural similarities and dissimilarities of the selected countries' export trade (Table 20).[11] It should be stressed that

Table 16

Export Shares 1963 - 1965

Percentages

Country Industry-group*	U.S.	Belgium	France	Germany	Italy	Nether-lands	(EEC-6)	U.K.	Sweden	Japan	Canada	TOTAL
5	24.88	3.55	7.19	20.69	5.41	8.68	(45.52)	14.10	3.18	10.07	2.26	100.0
6	26.33	3.95	11.43	21.79	6.18	6.67	(50.02)	12.64	1.48	5.67	3.87	100.0
7	28.75	2.65	12.68	20.40	5.57	6.52	(47.82)	17.76	1.34	3.02	1.30	100.0
24	20.65	3.80	15.03	15.49	7.74	4.63	(46.69)	16.63	3.31	11.22	1.49	100.0
10	50.54	5.51	6.68	3.42	4.09	7.19	(26.89)	13.23	0.18	0.24	8.90	100.0
11	22.36	4.20	9.03	28.69	5.91	0.92	(48.75)	19.72	2.71	4.12	2.33	100.0
12	4.75	1.52	7.31	15.31	3.52	7.94	(35.60)	6.64	17.14	35.18	0.69	100.0
15	9.64	16.19	13.79	20.06	4.11	3.55	(57.70)	9.71	4.49	15.32	3.14	100.0
16	16.92	14.69	6.29	10.75	2.29	3.31	(37.33)	13.79	2.24	2.56	27.16	100.0
17	18.53	5.61	8.50	23.64	6.88	2.49	(47.12)	15.01	4.38	12.87	2.08	100.0
19	28.37	0.90	5.83	27.20	3.78	2.85	(40.56)	12.11	1.44	12.55	4.95	100.0
20	31.37	2.30	6.31	25.07	6.16	2.23	(42.07)	16.23	4.00	3.36	2.97	100.0
22	22.92	4.31	18.09	4.74	5.78	17.31	(50.23)	13.23	1.47	4.38	7.78	100.0
23	9.42	9.25	13.48	11.34	15.49	6.78	(56.34)	14.51	1.20	17.56	0.97	100.0
26	15.47	13.21	11.10	20.56	7.80	3.78	(56.45)	13.49	1.67	11.80	1.11	100.0
27	19.59	3.69	6.83	8.18	2.67	5.20	(26.57)	9.27	12.80	2.78	29.00	100.0
28	12.45	4.43	7.41	9.05	4.19	3.12	(28.20)	3.04	16.64	7.63	32.05	100.0
30	22.21	5.84	9.78	18.85	6.43	5.25	(46.15)	13.97	3.69	8.25	5.72	100.0

Source: OECD, Trade by Commodities, Series B.

* The industry-group classification used here is that adopted by the OECD for compiling R&D statistics. It is elaborated in Table A.1 in Appendix A.

Table 17

Export Shares 1971 - 1973

Percentages

Country Industry-group*	U.S.	Belgium	France	Germany	Italy	Nether-lands	(EEC-6)	U.K.	Sweden	Japan	Canada	TOTAL
5	19.03	3.82	7.88	21.60	6.55	6.93	(46.78)	8.75	3.58	19.33	2.54	100.0
6	19.65	7.15	11.29	21.07	5.46	10.96	(55.94)	10.31	1.58	9.39	3.13	100.0
7	18.16	5.54	12.11	24.57	8.24	7.59	(58.05)	17.06	1.96	3.28	1.49	100.0
24	10.91	5.40	19.24	19.01	10.56	4.84	(59.05)	11.59	3.14	13.33	1.98	100.0
10	61.18	1.45	6.50	3.01	2.37	3.08	(16.41)	14.54	0.62	0.54	6.71	100.0
11	16.41	5.61	9.70	23.15	5.37	1.02	(44.85)	8.11	3.07	13.37	14.19	100.0
12	3.05	1.30	6.00	15.24	3.18	7.71	(33.43)	4.40	9.25	48.61	1.25	100.0
15	5.85	15.57	11.54	21.47	4.99	4.69	(58.26)	5.99	4.36	22.94	2.59	100.0
16	12.08	15.15	7.01	14.69	2.42	4.60	(43.87)	14.93	2.90	3.98	22.24	100.0
17	13.81	6.06	9.40	23.00	9.50	5.01	(52.97)	10.76	4.54	14.91	2.98	100.0
19	24.22	1.17	6.50	24.75	3.81	7.05	(43.28)	11.55	1.91	18.15	0.90	100.0
20	23.35	2.61	8.08	27.75	7.69	2.90	(49.03)	11.82	3.95	8.10	3.74	100.0
22	14.07	8.18	20.40	8.97	6.05	21.60	(65.20)	11.71	1.40	3.38	4.23	100.0
23	6.51	9.92	13.11	17.39	18.53	7.59	(66.54)	9.29	1.56	14.83	1.29	100.0
26	9.88	11.66	12.70	21.87	15.04	4.40	(65.67)	9.99	1.94	10.36	2.14	100.0
27	16.36	5.81	8.17	13.56	4.31	6.71	(38.29)	8.16	12.07	4.02	20.84	100.0
28	11.78	7.54	6.58	13.37	6.54	3.24	(37.27)	2.49	14.27	3.91	30.27	100.0
30	17.19	6.46	10.10	20.61	7.27	6.00	(50.44)	9.78	3.65	12.57	6.36	100.0

* Industry-group classification as per Table A.1, Appendix A.
Source: OECD, Trade by Commodities, Series B.

Table 18

Normalized Export Shares, 1963 - 1965

Country Industry-group*	U.S.	Belgium	France	Germany	Italy	Nether-lands	(EEC-6)	U.K.	Sweden	Japan	Canada
5	1.120	0.608	0.735	1.098	0.841	1.653	(0.986)	1.009	0.862	1.221	0.395
6	1.186	0.676	1.169	1.156	0.961	1.270	(1.084)	0.905	0.401	0.687	0.676
7	1.294	0.454	1.297	1.082	0.866	1.242	(1.036)	1.271	0.363	0.366	0.227
24	0.930	0.651	1.537	0.822	1.204	0.882	(1.012)	1.190	0.897	1.360	0.260
10	2.276	0.943	0.683	0.181	0.636	1.370	(0.583)	0.947	0.049	0.029	1.556
11	1.007	0.719	0.923	1.522	0.919	0.175	(1.056)	1.412	0.734	0.499	0.407
12	0.214	0.260	0.747	0.812	0.547	1.512	(0.771)	0.475	4.645	4.264	0.121
15	0.434	2.772	1.410	1.064	0.639	0.676	(1.250)	0.695	1.217	1.857	0.549
16	0.762	2.515	0.643	0.570	0.356	0.630	(0.809)	0.987	0.607	0.310	4.748
17	0.834	0.961	0.869	1.254	1.070	0.474	(1.021)	1.074	1.187	1.560	0.364
19	1.277	0.154	0.596	1.443	0.588	0.543	(0.879)	0.867	0.390	1.521	0.865
20	1.412	0.394	0.645	1.330	0.958	0.425	(0.912)	1.162	1.084	0.407	0.519
22	1.032	0.738	1.850	0.251	0.899	3.297	(1.088)	0.947	0.398	0.531	1.360
23	0.424	1.584	1.378	0.602	2.409	1.291	(1.221)	1.039	0.325	2.128	0.170
26	0.697	2.262	1.135	1.091	1.213	0.720	(1.223)	0.966	0.452	1.430	0.194
27	0.882	0.632	0.698	0.434	0.415	0.990	(0.576)	0.664	3.469	0.337	5.070
28	0.561	0.759	0.758	0.480	0.652	0.594	(0.611)	0.218	4.509	0.925	5.603
30	1.000	1.000	1.000	1.000	1.000	1.000	1.000	1.000	1.000	1.000	1.000

* Industry-group classification as per Table A.1, Appendix A.
Source: OECD, Trade by Commodities, Series B.

Table 19

Normalized Export Shares, 1971 - 1973

Country Industry-Group*	U.S.	Belgium	France	Germany	Italy	Nether-lands	(EEC-6)	U.K.	Sweden	Japan	Canada
5	1.107	0.591	0.780	1.048	0.901	1.155	(0.927)	0.895	0.981	1.538	0.399
6	1.143	1.107	1.118	1.022	0.751	1.827	(1.109)	1.054	0.433	0.747	0.492
7	1.056	0.858	1.199	1.192	1.133	1.265	(1.151)	1.744	0.537	0.261	0.234
24	0.635	0.836	1.905	0.922	1.453	0.807	(1.171)	1.185	0.860	1.060	0.311
10	3.559	0.224	0.644	0.146	0.326	0.513	(0.325)	1.487	0.170	0.043	1.055
11	0.955	0.868	0.960	1.123	0.739	0.170	(0.889)	0.829	0.841	1.064	2.231
12	0.177	0.201	0.594	0.739	0.437	1.285	(0.663)	0.450	2.534	3.867	0.197
15	0.340	2.410	1.143	1.042	0.686	0.782	(1.155)	0.612	1.195	1.825	0.407
16	0.703	2.395	0.694	0.713	0.333	0.767	(0.870)	1.527	0.794	0.317	3.497
17	0.803	0.938	0.931	1.116	1.307	0.835	(1.050)	1.100	1.244	1.186	0.469
19	1.409	0.181	0.644	1.201	0.524	1.175	(0.858)	1.181	0.523	1.444	0.142
20	1.358	0.404	0.800	1.346	1.058	0.483	(0.972)	1.209	1.082	0.644	0.588
22	0.818	1.266	2.020	0.435	0.832	3.600	(1.293)	1.197	0.384	0.269	0.665
23	0.379	1.536	1.298	0.844	2.549	1.265	(1.319)	0.950	0.427	1.180	0.203
26	0.575	1.805	1.257	1.061	2.069	0.733	(1.302)	1.022	0.531	0.824	0.336
27	0.952	0.899	0.809	0.658	0.593	1.118	(0.759)	0.834	3.307	0.320	3.277
28	0.685	1.167	0.651	0.649	0.900	0.540	(0.739)	0.255	3.910	0.311	4.759
30	1.000	1.000	1.000	1.000	1.000	1.000	1.000	1.000	1.000	1.000	1.000

* Industry-group classification as per Table A.1, Appendix A.
Source: OECD, Trade by Commodities, Series B.

Table 20

Relative R&D Intensities of Export Patterns:
Spearman Rank Correlations of Normalized Export
Shares with R&D Intensities of Product Groups.

Period Country	1963-1965	1971-1973
US	+0.67	+0.66
Belgium	-0.30	-0.62
France	-0.29	-0.36
FR Germany	+0.36	+0.37
Italy	-0.22	-0.33
Netherlands	+0.12	-0.13
(EEC-6)	(-0.06)	(-0.25)
U.K.	+0.32	+0.46
Sweden	-0.47	-0.37
Japan	-0.29	+0.05
Canada	-0.05	-0.22

Coefficients of 0.33 and 0.41 indicate significance at the 90 percent and 95 percent levels, respectively.

we are here discussing relative patterns of specialization; Belgian exports may appear heavily weighted toward traditional goods (textiles, food, etc.) relative to the United States, but they would probably appear heavily weighted in the other direction if Greece acted as the comparison. Furthermore, a trend toward relative specialization in traditional goods does not necessarily contradict the previous assertion that in absolute terms trade has become more concentrated in the more R&D-intensive product groups.

Table 20 suggests that, in the United States, West Germany and the United Kingdom, comparative advantage was relatively concentrated (in both periods) in R&D-intensive manufacture, in some contrast to Canada, EEC countries (excepting Germany), Sweden, and Japan. However, it appears that between 1963-1965 and 1971-1973, a considerable shift was taking place in relative specialization. Japanese and, to a lesser extent, Swedish and British export patterns were moving in the direction

Table 21

Relative R&D Intensities of Export Patterns (Intra-EEC Exports Excluded): Spearman Rank Correlations of Normalized Export Shares with R&D Intensities of Product-Groups

Period / Country	1963-1965	1971-1973
U.S.	+0.67	+0.57
Belgium	+0.08	-0.20
France	-0.21	-0.16
FR Germany	+0.47	+0.37
Italy	-0.33	-0.33
Netherlands	+0.19	+0.21
(EEC-6)	(+0.07)	(-0.08)
U.K.	+0.17	+0.25
Sweden	-0.55	-0.25
Japan	-0.36	+0.09
Canada	+0.05	-0.26

Coefficients of 0.33 and 0.41 indicate significance at the 90 percent and 95 percent levels, respectively.

of increasing R&D intensity, while EEC (Germany excepted) and Canadian export patterns were moving in the opposite direction, most emphatically in Belgium and the Netherlands.

The changes in EEC trading patterns are perhaps to be expected, given the Common Market's influence on trade in price-elastic goods. Removing intra-EEC tariff barriers greatly improved the competitive position of manufacturers of the more "traditional" goods, but had relatively little effect on comparative advantage in the manufacture of higher technology goods (for which price elasticity of demand tends to be relatively low). To avoid the bias induced by Common Market tariff protection, it is sensible to repeat the calculations in Table 20, this time excluding the intra-EEC trade of the EEC member countries. The results are shown in Table 21. With the exception of Belgium, the changes in the structure of extra-EEC exports were of no great significance, but it is notable on comparing Tables 20 and 21 that the Netherlands' extra-EEC exports were, by 1971-1973, considerably more R&D-intensive than its intra-EEC exports. The increasing R&D-intensity of Japanese and Swedish exports is again apparent.

NOTES

1. Woytinsky (1955) calculated that between 1867 and 1913 the values of world trade and production increased by 34 percent and 47 percent per decade, respectively; and by 20 percent and 37 percent between 1914 and 1938 (on average). From 1946 to 1952, production again outgrew trade, but thereafter the trend was reversed.

2. OECD Europe comprises the members of EFTA and the EEC, plus Greece, Portugal, Spain, and Turkey. Australia is the only country in the OECD outside the above-mentioned groups (it joined the OECD in 1971).

3. This trend was reciprocated by Canadian and Japanese exports to the United States. Between 1959 and 1966, their share of U.S. imports rose from 27 percent to 36 percent.

4. "Manufactured goods classified by materials": leather, rubber, wood and cork, paper, textile yarn, and fabrics, nonmetallic mineral manufactures, iron and steel, nonferrous metals, fabricated metal products. 'Other manufactures': furniture clothing, footwear, instruments, miscellaneous manufactured articles (including recording equipment).

5. The declining share of section 6 in the intra-OECD trade noted in Table 9 suggests that this trend continued in the 1960s.

6. Note that "matched structures" of exports and imports do not imply balance of trade by value.

7. One would also expect that if the Heckscher-Ohlin-Samuelson factor equalization theorem had some validity, the results in the real world would be to concentrate the search for competitive advantage more and more on product differentiation (broadly defined).

8. R&D-intensity is defined throughout this report as the ratio of R&D expenditure to value-added.

9. Exports have been aggregated over the three-year periods 1963-1965 and 1971-1973 to avoid errors that might arise from exceptional trading years.

10. These ten countries contributed approximately 89 percent of total OECD exports, 75 percent of world exports, of manufactured goods in 1972.

11. The ranking of industries according to R&D-intensity (company-funded) is as follows: 1 Aircraft; 2 Drugs; 3 Electricals; 4 Instruments; 5 Chemicals; 6 Mechanical machinery; 7 Nonferrous metals; 8 Motor vehicles; 9 Ferrous metals; 10 Ships; 11 Rubber, plastics, 12 Stone, clay, glass; 13 Fabricated metal prod-

ucts; 14 Food, drink, tobacco; 15 Textiles, leather, clothing; 16 Paper, printing; 17 Wood, furniture. This order was arrived at by calculating averages for each product group for the ten countries.

Problems arising from the use of R&D as a measure of innovative activity are discussed at length in Appendix B. Two points should be mentioned in this context. First, the proportion of expenditure on innovation accounted for by R&D differs from industry to industry. In chemicals, for instance, manufacturing start-up and other post-R&D activities account for the majority of innovative expenditures. A ranking according to "innovation-intensity" may therefore be rather different from the above. Second, the above ranking is an average—"R&D-intensity reversals" may result from industries being differently specialized from country to country.

Chapter IV

Innovation and Trading Performance: Statistical Tests

PREAMBLE

The statistical exercises carried out in the previous chapter illustrated the changing patterns of exports from the ten major OECD countries in recent years. Hufbauer's study (1970), in which he tested the ability of different theories to explain the product structures of exports and imports in a selection of OECD countries, has already been referred to. Gruber and Vernon (1970) and Hirsch (1974) used similar methodologies and reached similar conclusions. Gruber, Mehta and Vernon's study (1967) looked specifically at associations between R&D-intensities of U.S. manufacture and the structure of U.S. trade, and its similarities and dissimilarities when compared with the structure of French, German, and British exports.

This line of inquiry is intended to reveal the location of comparative advantage in an economy at a given moment in time. Restricted as it is to a purely static picture of international trade, its predictive powers in relation to temporal movements in economic activity are limited. Indeed, unless handled carefully, it can mislead. According to Tables 18 and 19, the United Kingdom had, in the 1960s, a comparative advantage in research-intensive product groups like aircraft and mechanical machinery, while France had an advantage in more traditional industries like food and textiles. However, if one compares the movement of French and British trade shares in, for instance, mechanical machinery, it is apparent that the French industry prospered while the British industry declined (relatively). By inferring "comparative advantage" from a static picture, one is limited to comparing the *structures* of different countries' export trade; one is not justified in anticipating the way in which trade shares will change over time.

A further limitation of this approach is that it gives no insight into the dynamic influence of innovation on the fortunes of competing industries. It does not tell us whether different levels of innovative effort in, say, the electrical industry will bring about a reallocation of production of electrical goods between countries over a period of time.

Should we expect innovation to lead to international shifts in competitive advantage?

As was discussed earlier, the neoclassical model predicts that production will be allocated in accordance with the factor endowments of trading nations. At time t_1, U.S. factor endowments (capital, labor, and land) relative to those of other countries result in a commodity composition of manufacture, which will be reflected in its pattern of exports. These relative endowments will lead the United States to have x_1 percent of world trade in commodity C_1, x_2 percent of trade in commodity C_2, and so on.

Assuming t_1 represents (approximately) an equilibrium position, at time t_2 these shares of trade will be unchanged, provided there has been no exogenous change in relative factor endowments. In equilibrium, if relative endowments of capital, labor, and land remain unaltered with the passage of time, there is no reason to expect shifts in trade shares.

In this respect, R&D, if regarded as a factor of production, behaves quite differently. By generating new opportunities for expanding production (opportunities that are uniquely held by the innovating country), innovation can bring about an *increase* in the parent country's trade share, and a corresponding decrease in the share of competitors. Innovation is constructive to the innovator, destructive to his competitor. Furthermore, the innovator can sell his new product/process at monopoly prices, leading to profit which can be invested in further creative (and destructive) activities, reinforcing the innovator's acquired comparative advantage. Innovation will lead in certain industries to a concentration of production in the country that gives it highest priority (for whatever reason), and is best able to marshal productive resources in order to profit from the new knowledge.

This is oversimplified, but it does suggest that innovation has a disruptive effect on trade shares; this is in line with the picture of industrial development outlined in Chapter II

One point should, however, be made clear. Increases and decreases in trade shares are synonymous with relatively fast or slow rates of growth in the manufacture of exportable goods. We noted in the previous chapter the wide variation in growth rates, even though the postwar growth in export trade was experienced to a greater or lesser extent by all OECD countries.

These discrepancies in growth rates, have, of course, been widely debated by theorists of economic growth since 1945 (and equally widely ignored by international trade theorists). So intractable have been the problems of handling and ascribing weights to large numbers of variables (economic and otherwise), and of disentangling cause and effect, that progress has been slow and the debate inconclusive. In the United Kingdom the argument has been polarized between those who believe that factor shortages have been the major constraint on economic growth and those who believe the constraint to have been a lack of competitiveness in the international marketplace. These opinions carry with them contrasting views of the direction of causation beween export growth and domestic economic growth—the former believing that domestic economic growth is a precondition for export growth, the latter believing that growth in export trade is a precondition for domestic economic growth.[1]

It should be recognized that we are here taking sides with those who regard international competitiveness as the controlling element in export and domestic economic growth (and hence in movements in trade shares), but with one important difference. By "competitiveness," the growth economists normally imply price competitiveness, and the only role allotted to technical change lies in the increase in labor productivity arising from investment in new process technologies. The part played by product and process innovation in determining international competitiveness in a large segment of the modern industrial economy has generally been ignored. It is seldom realized that innovation has a dual impact on economic development: it increases productivity in the purchasing industry, but it also generates opportunities for the innovator to expand (or maintain) his trading activities at home and abroad.

We wish to test the hypothesis that industrial innovation has a disruptive effect on trade shares for the industry groups listed in Tables 16–19. As discussed previously, one would expect innovative effort to be more influential in some industries (e.g., chemicals) than in others (e.g., textiles). Taking an industry at a time, innovative effort in that industry will be ranked across countries, and correlated with a measure indicating relative changes in trade shares over the selected time period (1963–1973).

It should be stressed that this is a quite different approach from that adopted previously. In case there should be any confusion, rankings of innovative effort and trading performance in a hypothetical industry may be illustrated as follows:

	U.S.	Belgium	France	Germany	Italy
Innovative effort	2	8	5	1	10
Trading performance	3	4	7	5	2

	Netherlands	U.K.	Sweden	Japan	Canada
Innovative effort	3	7	6	4	9
Trading performance	1	9	10	6	8

There remains the problem of measurement. How are the two variables, "innovativeness" and "trading performance," to be measured? Do sufficiently reliable, internationally comparable statistics exist to permit such an analysis? These issues are discussed at length in Appendices A and B. It is important that the difficulties should be clearly understood: the assumption of perfect measures and statistics too frequently leads to exaggerated claims for the theoretical value of statistical tests.

R&D-intensities (R&D/value added) have been chosen as the measures of innovative effort. R&D-intensities of manufacture for the ten major

OECD countries, and across fifteen product groups, are set out in Table A.5 in Appendix A. The main snags attending the use of this measure arise from R&D being an input, not an output measure; from R&D being only partially representative of the resources needed to launch new or improved products and processes onto the marketplace; from variations in industrial specialization across countries; from the imperfect statistics that have made some estimation necessary, and have made it impossible to build in an adequate time lag between R&D expenditure and commercial exploitation.

As regards the measurement of trading performance, the main problem arises from the large variation in the scale of the export trade of the selected countries. This introduces a distortion into any measure that is difficult to eradicate: if the measure is designed on the basis of arithmetical differences, the performance of the larger trading nations will be overrated; if it is designed on the basis of ratios (or growth rates), it induces a bias in the opposite direction. For this reason, correlations will be carried out with measures of trading performance based on both differences (R_D) and ratios (r_s and R_S); and the summation ($R_S + R_D$) can be regarded as an attempt to cancel out the respective biases. These measures we discuss in Appendix B.

It is up to the reader to judge whether the imperfections described in Appendices A and B invalidate the following analysis. It should also be borne in mind that statistical tests are only able to *in*validate hypotheses; they may suggest that statistical data are consistent with an image of (in this case) industrial development derived from empirical observations, but this does not amount to validation. As such, the next pages do not provide us with a definitive "test" of the hypotheses outlined in Chapter II; they can only add to, or subtract from, our confidence in their general merit.

RESULTS OF STATISTICAL TESTS

The outcome of correlating R&D-intensities (as set out in Table A.5) with the various measures of trading performance are shown in Table 22. Values of 0.44, 0.55, and 0.73 indicate significance at the 90 percent, 95 percent and 99 percent levels, respectively.[2]

After all the talk of imperfections and possible sources of error, the strengths of the correlation coefficients in Table 22 are encouraging.

Table 22

Spearman Rank Correlation Coefficients of R&D Intensities Correlated with:

Industry-group*		Normalized ratios of export differences (R_D)	Ratios of shares (r_S)	Normalized ratios of export shares (R_S)	Sum of normalized ratios ($R_S + R_D$)
5	(a)	+0.35	-0.50	-0.42	+0.13
	(b)	-0.12	-0.67	-0.33	-0.01
6,24	(a)	+0.45	+0.83	+0.75	+0.52
7	(a)	+0.35	+0.52	+0.60	+0.53
	(b)	+0.34	+0.53	+0.60	+0.53
10	(b)	–	+0.86	+0.82	–
11	(a)	-0.45	-0.70	-0.72	-0.85
12	(a)	+0.01	-0.30	-0.16	+0.03
15	(a)	+0.43	+0.37	+0.49	+0.54
16	(a)	+0.24	+0.28	-0.25	+0.19
17	(a)	-0.09	-0.12	-0.04	+0.14
19	(a)	+0.31	+0.42	+0.59	+0.46
	(b)	+0.23	+0.27	+0.55	+0.46
20	(a)	-0.09	-0.32	-0.24	+0.03
	(b)	+0.18	-0.31	-0.36	+0.05
22	(a)	-0.18	-0.28	-0.18	+0.02
23	(a)	-0.10	-0.48	-0.38	-0.20
26	(a)	-0.25	-0.64	-0.47	-0.42
27,28	(a)	+0.36	-0.47	-0.58	+0.20

(a) : Company-funded R&D (b): Total R&D
* Industry-group classification as per Table A.1

Whichever measure of trading performance we take, the industries fall into three distinct groups, whereby R&D-intensities and trading performance are:

(a) Positively correlated:	Aircraft Chemicals, rubber, and plastics Drugs Ferrous metals Instruments
(b) Poorly correlated:	Electricals Ships Nonferrous metals Fabricated metal products Mechanical machinery Food, drink, tobacco Textiles Paper, printing, wood
(c) Negatively correlated:	Motor vehicles Stone, clay, glass

It has already been pointed out that the direction of causation between innovative effort and trading performance is not unequivocal. Let us for the moment assume that causation is straightforward—that innovative effort influences, but is independent of, trading performance. In which case, how closely do the above results comply with expectations? This assumption will be relaxed in later paragraphs, under the heading "Influence of Economic Performance."

Given uniform causality, it would appear that, in four R&D-intensive industries (chemicals, aircraft, drugs, instruments), innovative effort had a strong influence on shifting patterns of trade in the time period in question, in line with our predictions; the ferrous metals industry, usually classified as "traditional," is an interesting addition to this list. The two remaining research-intensive industries—electricals and mechanical machinery—show no clear association between innovation and changes in trade shares. Nor do the majority of "traditional" industries, as expected. In all R&D-intensive industries, government funding makes only a modest difference to the coefficients; if anything, it decreases the strength of the correlations. Finally, in the motor vehicle and stone, clay and glass industries, low R&D-intensity appears to be associated with good trading performance.

These results emphasize an earlier point—that attempts to build "general models" of industrial behavior in order to explain trading patterns are likely to be abortive.

To what extent can these inter-industry differences be explained without recourse to micro-studies? In particular, why do the R&D-intensive electrical and mechanical machinery industries not conform to the expected pattern? It is worthwhile starting with some general remarks on the problems posed by foreign investment and licensing.

Foreign Investment, Licensing and Trade

Any examination of international economic relations should strictly consider international trade, foreign direct investment, and licensing together as alternative (or even complementary) responses to particular competitive conditions. A firm that has a comparative advantage over its competitors as a result of its unique stock of technological knowledge may exploit it in different ways, depending on market conditions at home and abroad, and on its own commercial strategies (short- and long-term). It may expand production at home and export abroad; it may invest overseas and compete from within foreign markets (especially if tariff barriers, quotas or preferential purchasing limit export possibilities); it may license the technology to foreign producers. If it follows either of the last two options there may be a gain or loss in export trade (normally the latter), depending on the context.

This raises the question as to whether trade on its own can be considered as a proxy for comparative advantage. In the 1960s, U.S. industries in particular invested large sums in overseas production, to the extent that the volume of production by U.S. affiliates in Europe is now substantially greater than the volume of exports from the United States to Europe. The ideal proxy would be a measure that incorporated all three alternatives unfortunately, it is virtually impossible to construct such a measure, given the dearth of information outside the United States relating to multinational production and licensing.[3]

The problem is, in fact, more serious when a "static" analysis (of the Gruber, Mehta and Vernon type) of a country's trading performance is used to determine areas of comparative advantage. Trade statistics may, for instance, "reveal" that a competitive industry is uncompetitive in world markets (relative to other industries in the same country), the reason being that it prefers to exploit its advantage by investing in production facilities overseas.

Provided the commercial preferences of the innovating industry (as between exporting, overseas production and licensing) are similar at both ends of the time period in question, trade statistics will provide us with an adequate proxy for its international performance. If our assertions are correct, innovative effort will be reflected in changes in trade shares and, for that matter, in changes in the volume of overseas investment and licensing (for the industry/country in question).[4] However, this is relevant only to "donor" countries—those that are exporting the results of their R&D, by whatever means—and not to "acceptors." Where industries rely heavily on imported technology, performing little R&D themselves, it is possible that large increases in trade shares will be associated with little innovative effort. This is especially the case where countries are being used by multinational companies as bases from which to export to protected markets (e.g., U.S. pharmaceutical firms exporting from a manufacturing base in Eire); or where relatively cheap labor and capital are being exploited in the manufacture of subassemblies (e.g., the U.S. car industry manufacturing in Canada).[5]

Our correlations should, therefore, sort out industries where, by and large, indigenous innovation is a precondition for good national performance in world markets (e.g., the aircraft industry and, if we could disaggregate to that level, the textile machinery industry); from those in which a strong trading position can be built upon the import of foreign technology (e.g., the Canadian motor vehicle industry)—albeit temporarily.

Industries With Expected Correlation Coefficients

For the aircraft, chemical (including rubber and plastics), drug, and instrument industries, the positive associations between R&D-intensity and changes in trade shares (however measured) are as expected. In the case of instruments, the correlation coefficients indicate significance at the 90 percent level; in drugs and chemicals significance is closer to the 95 percent level; and in aircraft correlations are significant at the 99 percent level.

These are all "innovation-intensive" industries, in which the monopoly power afforded by their products and processes are essential to competitive survival (and expansion) in world markets. As discussed previously, the Schumpeterian "creative destruction" of competing industries leads us to anticipate that innovation will have a dynamic influence on market shares.

The results for the so-called "traditional industries"—ships, nonferrous metals, fabricated metal products, food and drink, textiles and clothing, paper and wood—are also in line with expectations (ferrous metals excepted). Here relative costs and availabilities of labor, capital and land, and the efficiency with which they are used, take on a much greater significance, and the relatively minor expenditures on R&D are unlikely to have a major impact on trading performance. However, one would not wish to give an impression of unchanging production techniques in these industries. On the contrary, the postwar years have seen revolutions in many of the production processes employed in "traditional" manufacture (see Figure 2 for evidence of dramatic changes in one sector).[6] R&D is largely "imported" in these industries—embodied in capital goods and materials.

Industries With Unexpected Correlation Coefficients

The results for the four remaining industries require rather more explanation: the positive correlation between innovative effort and trading performance in the ferrous metals industry; the poor correlations for the electrical and mechanical engineering industries; and the strong negative correlation for the motor-vehicle industry.

(a) Ferrous metals: The ferrous-metal industry is not a research-intensive industry, as normally defined. R&D expenditures for the ten OECD countries range from 0.3 percent (Italy) to 2.5 percent (Netherlands) of value-added. While innovation is undoubtedly important in the industry (especially in developing and improving new processes), one would not have thought it played as central a role in industrial competition as in the more research-intensive industries.

There are three possible explanations for the apparent relationship between innovative effort and trading performance in this industry.

First, that we have underestimated the impact of innovation in this industry in the past; in particular that product differentiation and product quality are rather more important than previously recognized. Second, that R&D-intensities are acting as "proxies" for progressive attitudes which are also reflected in high levels of investment and a general willingness to adopt modern production practices, which in turn lead to successful trading. Third, we cannot ignore the possibility that it is a chance association.

(b) Motor Vehicles: Rankings of trading performance and R&D-intensity in the motor-vehicle industry are set out in Table 23. The strong negative correlation is largely the result of apparently high innovative effort in the Netherlands and Italy (with poor trading results) and low innovative effort in Belgium, Canada, and Japan (with good trading results).

In the absence of empirical studies of innovation in the car industry (it has been curiously neglected by researchers), it would perhaps be foolish to attempt an explanation. It is the strength of the negative correlation coefficient that is so unexpected. The reasons may lie in the unreliable R&D statistics (especially with regard to the Netherlands) or in the heavy foreign investment that characterized the industry in the 1960s. The U.S. industry, in particular, was involved in large-scale production transfers in this period, the recipients being mainly Canada and Belgium (the British and Germans also invested in Belgium). It is striking in Table A.5 that Belgian and Canadian R&D-intensities in this industry were well below those of other countries.

(c) Electrical and Mechanical Machinery: The unexpected results recorded for the electrical and mechanical machinery industries provide us with the main puzzle.

There is a statistical problem influencing the results for the above two industries that we have not mentioned yet: *trade* in computers is registered as a subcategory of mechanical machinery (office equipment), while computer *R&D* is included by some countries with electricals (e.g., the United Kingdom), by others with mechanical machinery (e.g., the United States). While trade in computers is a fairly minor proportion of total trade in mechanical machinery, computer R&D will always constitute a substantial proportion of R&D expenditures in whichever category it is included. Without a detailed breakdown of computer R&D ex-

Table 23

Rankings of Trading Performance ($R_S + R_D$), and R&D-Intensity

Industry	Measure / Country	U.S.	Belgium	France	Germany	Italy	Netherlands	U.K.	Sweden	Japan	Canada
Electricals	$R_S + R_D$	3	9	6	5	4	8	7	2	1	10
	R&D intensity	5	8	6	3	10	2	4	1	9	9
	d^2	4	1	0	4	36	36	9	1	64	1
Mechanical machinery	$R_S + R_D$	4	10	6	1	5	9	3	7	2	8
	R&D-intensity	2	7	9	5	10	1	4	3	6	8
	d^2	4	9	9	16	25	64	1	16	16	0
Motor vehicles	$R_S + R_D$	6	3	5	7	8	10	9	4	2	1
	R&D-intensity	2	10	6	4	3	1	5	7	8	9
	d^2	16	49	1	9	25	81	16	9	36	64

penditures from country to country, we are unfortunately unable to compensate for this statistical imperfection.

Leaving aside computers, the electrical industry covers a large range of very different products, from heavy electrical machinery to television sets, from electronic components to cables. In three respects this diversity may lead to poor statistical associations between R&D and trade: the R&D-intensities of production vary considerably from product to product (different thresholds); behavior with regard to the location of production differs from product group to product group (e.g., in heavy electrical equipment, there is little transfer of production, but quite extensive licensing; in television, off-shore production is commonplace); and the rates of growth of trade in the different commodities may vary, so that it is possible that exports of low R&D-intensity products grow faster than exports of high R&D-intensity products, leading to a poor statistical fit between innovative effort and trade. In comparison, the "product mixes" of the chemical, drug, and instrument industries are more homogeneous.

Rankings of trading performance and R&D-intensity in the electrical industry are shown in Table 23. The poor correlation is due mainly to the good trading performance of the Italian and Japanese industries, achieved with relatively low innovative effort, and to the poor trading performance of the Dutch industry. This may be explained either by the Italian and Japanese willingness to import technology and exploit their labor-cost advantages, in contrast with the Dutch tendency to perform R&D at home and produce multinationally; or by differential rates of growth of high and low R&D-intensity products (the Dutch specializing in the former, the Italians and Japanese in the latter).

In an attempt to break into this problem, trade in electricals has been divided into two groups—the one characterized by high R&D-intensity, the other by low R&D-intensity (according to our estimation).[7] Correlating sums of normalized ratios (Rs + Rd) for these groups with the ranking of R&D-intensity given in Table A.5 yields Spearman Rank correlation coefficients of −0.02 and −0.01, respectively—hardly any difference (one might have expected the high R&D-intensity group to have given a positive correlation coefficient). Furthermore, the rankings of export performance for the two groups was not significantly different; Japan, for instance, ranked first in trading performance in both high and low R&D-intensity product groups. Rates of growth of trade in the two groupings were also approximately equal.

Perhaps these results are not too surprising. The poor correlation for the low R&D-intensity product group is to be expected, given the influence of low labor costs on the location of production. And the imperfect markets for electrical power machinery and switchgear, and telecommunications equipment (preferential procurement being common practice in countries with these industries) would account for the apparent lack of association between innovative effort and changes in trade shares in the high R&D-intensity product groups.

Poor statistics, factor mobility, and imperfect markets probably explain the results for the electrical industry. The poor correlations recorded for the mechanical engineering industry are less easily explained. The competitive behavior of the textile machinery industry described in Chapter II is fairly typical, although not general, of the industry as a whole: little factor mobility; high skill-intensity of manufacture; importance of external economics; small- to medium-sized companies, but with many oligopolistic characteristics; and the search for monopoly powers via the development of new and improved products.

One could therefore expect this industry in particular to exhibit a close association between innovative effort and changes in trade shares. How are we to explain the poor correlations in Table 22? Have we exaggerated the importance of innovation in this industry?

Again, inadequate R&D statistics are the most probable reason. With the large numbers of firms in each country, the coverage of R&D surveys in this industry tends to be less comprehensive than, for instance, in the more concentrated chemical industry (especially in countries which have had difficulties with their data collection—e.g., France and Germany). The rankings of R&D-intensity (first) and trading performance (ninth) for the Netherlands also contributed substantially to the poor correlation (see Table 23); it is possible that our estimations of Dutch R&D expenditures in this industry are wide of the mark. The additional problems presented by the inclusion or exclusion of computer R&D have already been mentioned.

It should also be remembered that a substantial part of innovative effort in the mechanical engineering industry—design engineering—falls outside the Frascati definition of R&D; one may not be justified in using R&D as a proxy for innovative input in this industry.

Influence of Economic Performance on Innovative Effort

So far in this section we have considered a line of causation running from innovation to economic performance. It is quite possible that levels of innovative effort—and the types of product or process the firm chooses to develop—may be influenced by historical performance and by demand expectations within the national and international economies.[8] Since we have been unable to build adequate time lags between R&D and economic output into our statistical tests, this may be a more plausible reason for the statistical associations outlined above. There may be a link, direct or indirect, between the rate of growth of demand within an economy and the intensity with which firms develop new technologies, equivalent (analogous?) to the well-documented links between economic growth and investment rates. The recent decline in company-funded R&D noted in the United States and the United Kingdom, coinciding with downturns in the two economies, suggests that such a connection does indeed exist.

This is an area that has been little researched. Studies carried out in the United States suggest that some companies "peg" their R&D expenditures to the level of their turnover, and that R&D sales ratios are widely imitated by companies with equivalent technological specializations.[9] This seems too simple an explanation, implying that expenditure on technical change is independent, or at least loosely dependent, on the prevailing economic environment. Studies are needed to compare the behavior of companies situated in different national economies.

In the absence of a reliable theory, we can only surmise the possible ways in which the economic environment (and perceptions of its future development) impinges on a firm's decisions in relation to the resources it devotes to technical change. The following may be relevant:

(a) The pressure for labor-saving devices—and for devices extending production capabilities—is likely to be more intense in the fast-growing than in the slow-growing economy, as labor becomes scarcer and more expensive in relation to capital.

(b) Venture capital will tend to be plentiful, and available to both buyers and sellers of new and improved technologies, when market demand is expected to grow rapidly in both the short- and long-term.

(c) Three types of capital expenditure are sometimes distinguished in the literature: capital widening, which is aimed at expanding productive capacity, and involves the purchase of capital goods identical with or at least closely similar to those already employed by the firm; capital deepening, which increases the capital-intensity of production by substituting capital for labor (output remaining unchanged in both quantity and quality); and innovational investment, the capital expenditure associated with product and/or process innovation.

Lamfalussy (1961) has argued that firms will partake in all three types of investment, whether they are facing growing, stagnant, or declining demand for their products; but that the balance struck between them varies with demand expectations (in particular) as well as with the predicted availability and price of the appropriate factors of production. This will be reflected in both the quantity and quality of innovation undertaken. In a slow-growing economy there will be a strong bias toward the continued use of well-tried techniques, and where innovation takes place it will tend to be relatively incremental and cost-saving; in a fast-growing economy, there will be an emphasis on the construction of major new plants, and innovation will in contrast be more radical and expansion-oriented.

(d) Attitudes towards risk vary according to the historical experience of the entrepreneurial class. Self-confidence engenders, and is engendered by, successful economic performance.

Together these could add up to a causal link existing between growth rates and R&D intensities, within a given industry. However, it is perhaps most realistic to regard economic performance and the level (and quality) of innovative effort as being mutually reinforcing. As so often in economic growth theory, a country may find itself trapped in a vicious or virtuous circle: slow growth induces low expectations and hence low investment (innovational or otherwise), raises relative costs per unit of output and slows down technical progress, which in turn reduces the price- and technological competitiveness of exportable goods, lowering future expectations of industrial expansion; whereas fast growth leads to high expectations and investment, increases productivity and technical progress, enhances international competitiveness and thereby once again raises future expectations. As we know only too well in the United Kingdom, once a country has fallen off the roundabout it is extraordinarily difficult to regain a secure foothold.

NOTES

1. The best-known expositions of these contrasting viewpoints are by Kaldor (1966) and Beckerman (1965). Kaldor, however, has since retracted and now regards low competitiveness as the main cause of Britain's economic decline.

2. The sample was limited to seven for the aircraft industry: Germany, Japan, and Sweden were excluded as political circumstances limited production (in Japan and Germany) and trade (in Sweden) in this area until very recently. The result nevertheless indicates significance at the 99 percent level. $R_S + R_D$ could not be calculated as the volume of Belgian and Canadian trade declined, giving negative values. For the aircraft industry we have only considered total R&D expenditures. This has obvious pitfalls, but in Europe governments subsidize the great majority of R&D, military or civilian; company-funded R&D is relatively insignificant.

The analysis would in general have benefited from a larger sample of countries, including, for instance, Austria, Denmark, Norway, and Switzerland. Shortage of time prevented us from undertaking the arduous task of compiling data for these countries; besides which the quality of their R&D statistics is rather poor—especially with regard to Switzerland.

3. Horst (1972) attempted this for U.S./Canadian interchanges, and found that his composite measure gave a better indication of comparative advantage than exports.

4. Between 1963-1965 and 1971-1973, it seems reasonable to assume that drastic shifts in preference did not occur in our selected countries. This is not to say that preferences did not vary considerably from country to country, and from industry to industry.

5. In both cases, large exports will frequently be associated with large imports of unfinished goods.

6. For these reasons, it could be argued that the neoclassical model is as inapplicable to the "traditional" industries as it is to the "advanced technology" industries.

7. The two groups are as follows: high R&D-intensity: electrical power machinery and switchgear; telecommunications equipment; medical electrical equipment; valves, transistors, ICs; electrical measuring and control instruments; accelerators; Low R&D-intensity: TVs; radios; cables and insulators; domestic electrical equipment; batteries and accumulators; lamps; automotive electrical equipment; and "other electricals."

8. We are here referring to industry-financed R&D alone.

9. The literature on this subject has been reviewed by Falk (1974).

Chapter V

Final Comments

The range of problems to which the neoclassical theory of international trade may be applied is strictly limited within the modern economic system. Based as it is on the "assumption" that economic systems are self-regulating—that their natural condition is one of equilibrium and political tranquillity—the neoclassical theory does not recognize the *de*-stabilizing effect that technical change (deliberately induced) has on international trading patterns.

The product-cycle theory only partially contradicts neoclassical orthodoxy. While it acknowledges the important part played by product innovation in deciding the location of production (in the innovation-intensive industrial sectors), it nevertheless regards the development of a new product as a temporary dislocation to the status quo, to be followed in time by a return to orthodoxy as the technology stabilizes and becomes common property. It is perhaps for this reason that economists have had little difficulty in reconciling the product cycle and neoclassical theories.

We have argued in this book that the product-cycle theory is inappropriate to a substantial part of the modern industrial system. It is particularly inappropriate to the capital-goods industries where there is scant historical evidence of technical standardization bringing about the predicted relocation of production. Faced in most industrially advanced countries by an insatiable demand for labor-saving devices, firms have been able to maintain control in the marketplace by continually updating and improving their original innovations, as well as by developing radically new techniques.

Statistical tests in this paper have supported the viewpoint that innovation has a dynamic impact on the survival and growth of firms, although we have to tread cautiously given imperfect measures and statistics. An injection of Schumpeterian ideas could do much to revitalize trade theory. Much could also be gained by carrying out detailed *technological* studies of the evolution of products and processes, which could provide the backbone for a more realistic economic analysis.

However, no less pressing is the need to improve our understanding of the relationships between a firm's propensity to innovate, its historical economic performance, and the general economic environment, internal and external to the firm. How, for instance, do expectations of growth in demand impinge on both the quantity and quality of innovation undertaken by the firm? To what extent do factor shortages within the firm encourage or inhibit the development and introduction of new techniques—and the firm's penetration of world markets? How does a firm's overall productive efficiency affect on the one hand its innovativeness, on the other hand its ability to profit from its innovations? Until we can answer such questions our understanding of the radical shifts in economic power that have taken place within the OECD since 1945 will be seriously limited.

Appendix A

The Measurement of Industrial Innovation

A simplified model of the development of a new product in an industrial firm may be drawn as follows:

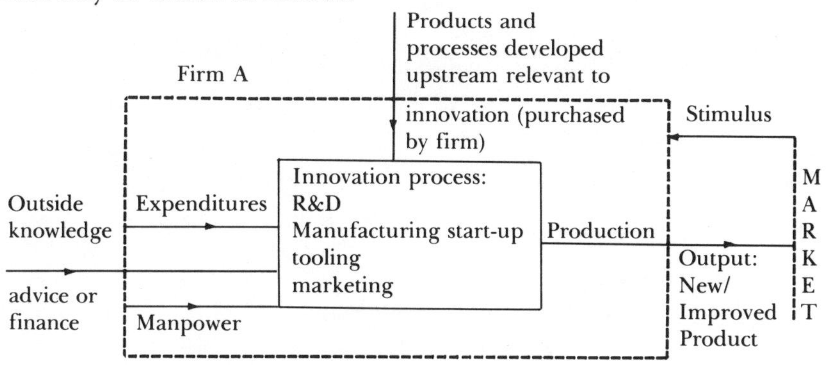

How is the "innovative performance" of the firm to be measured?

Ideally, one would wish to have a complete record of both inputs to, and outputs from, the firm's efforts to innovate. However, it has proved in practice difficult, if not impossible, to measure outputs, while *some* of the inputs (usually the major ones) can be measured with fair accuracy.

The problems of measuring outputs are discussed at some length by Freeman (1970). He identifies patents, published scientific articles, and physical evidence of new products or techniques as useful but only partial indicators of innovative output. In general, outputs can be measured with relative ease at the micro-level—when one is concerned with a particular development program, or with the innovative record of a particular firm. At the macro-level, only patents offer practical possibilities of aggregation, but they are notoriously difficult to interpret and are of variable significance from industry to industry.

Consequently, we are forced to consider the usefulness of input measures (especially R&D expenditures and manpower) as a "surrogate" for outputs. Industrial innovation is not the only area in which this approach had been adopted: expenditures on education, medicine, and many other social services are used as approximate indicators of their effectiveness. However, as we shall see later, this approach has to be treated with great care; in particular, implicit in the term is some conception of the meaning and form of the output.

In assessing the validity of the surrogate, two questions have to be answered:

(a) Is the selected input measure (in our case, R&D) appropriate and "representative," given the variety of other activities contributing to the output?
(b) Can we assume that the level of input will be reflected in the level of output—that some form of "production function" can be formulated relating inputs to outputs?

R&D as a Measure of Innovative Activity

Here we consider (a) above.

R&D is defined in the OECD Frascati Manual as "creative work undertaken on a systematic basis to increase the stock of scientific and technical knowledge and to use this stock of scientific and technical knowledge to devise new applications." As such, R&D is a necessary, but not sufficient, step in the so-called "innovation process"; it is the creative (technologically) prerequisite for launching a new product on the marketplace.[1] Parallel and subsequent to the R&D phase, engineering drawings have to be prepared, jigs and tools manufactured or bought in, the market analyzed, advertising campaigns planned, and so on.

The proportion of total innovation costs taken up by R&D depends on the technology being developed. Studies by Mansfield (1971) in the United States and Stead (1975) in Canada have illustrated the variation in innovation cost structures from industry to industry. Taking an average of their results, R&D comprised 30 percent, 46 percent and 64 percent of total innovation costs in the chemical, mechanical machinery, and electrical industries, respectively.[2] Naturally, these are statistical averages; proportions will vary from project to project according to managerial choice and the technologies in question.

Thus, identical R&D expenditures in different industries do not necessarily indicate identical expenditures on innovation taken as a whole. Mansfield's and Stead's findings suggest that $1 million spent on R&D in the chemical and electrical industries indicate total innovation expenditures of $3.3 million and $1.5 million, respectively. Comparisons of levels of R&D expenditure between *different* industries are thus to be treated with caution, if the purpose is to compare levels of innovative activity. One is, however, justified in using R&D as an indicator of innovative activity when considering equivalent industries at home or abroad—comparing like with like. That the German chemical industry is more R&D-intensive than its U.K. counterpart can be taken as evidence of greater innovative effort, assuming that the Germans are devoting their resources to technologies with the same R&D costs as the British.[3]

This last assumption is important. Different R&D-intensities could be a reflection of the German and British industries being differently specialized (or having different ambitions), not of the relative "obsessiveness" with which they develop equivalent products or processes; they would indicate qualitative, not quantitative, differences in innovative effort. To give a simple example, if industry A entirely specializes in NC machine tools, and industry B in conventional milling machines, the cost of developing new products (or new models of old products) will be considerably higher in industry A than in industry B; industry A will be more R&D-intensive than industry B—the threshold of R&D activity it will have to exceed to remain technologically competitive will be higher than for industry B. Thus to compare the R&D-intensities of industries A and B is only informative insofar as an indication is given of differing industrial specializations (although this may in itself be of considerable interest). Only by comparing industry A_1 with industry A_2—both NC machine-tool producers—can we draw conclusions concerning links between levels of R&D expenditure and trading performance.

To give a cross-country example, it would be hazardous to use R&D-intensities as a basis for an analysis of the competitive performance of the Irish and U.K. electrical industries, given that the Irish are producing a limited range of "light" electrical equipment, while the British are involved with heavy electrical machinery and transformers, computers, and other inherently more expensive technologies.

As we shall later be using R&D-intensities as proxies for levels of innovative activity (ranking them across countries) it is important that we should be aware of the extent to which the above assumption is valid for the industries and countries being considered. In general, we can say that it is most likely to be valid if the countries under consideration have equivalent per capita income levels, demanding equivalent types of product, and that domestic industries are equally diversified to satisfy these demands. It will be least valid if production is significantly specialized (and the technologies in question have different threshold levels) country by country in particular industry groups.

In the previous section, evidence was put forward to suggest that production within the various product groups *is* very considerably specialized, even at a high level of disaggregation. This can be regarded as a logical outcome of the search for monopoly powers via innovation that we discussed earlier. We have to consider whether, taking for instance the chemical industry, concentration on different technologies in the United States and France will still result in equivalent *average* R&D thresholds. To use an analogy, will mixing different wavelengths of light, of differing strengths, result in the same shade of brown?

To tackle this question we would need a detailed knowledge of technological specializations from country to country, plus empirical evidence of R&D thresholds. At the macro-level, it is extremely difficult, but perhaps we can take comfort from having chosen the OECD countries with the most diversified industrial structures as our statistical sample. Specialization may be rife within these countries, but it will be less evident on aggregation than if we had included less industrialized countries. Thus the technological "spread" of the German, French, and U.K. electrical industries is more likely to be equivalent than that of the U.K., Spanish, and Irish industries.

While we shall proceed on the assumption that industries are technologically equivalent in our ranking of R&D-intensities (and innovative output), we do nevertheless recognize this as an important source of error. Unfortunately, it would take another study to assess the validity of this assumption. It should be stressed, however, that even if specialization seriously affects relative R&D-intensities, it is still intrinsically interesting to know that country A (high R&D-intensity) is giving higher priority to relatively sophisticated technologies than country B (low R&D-intensity).

Innovative Output as a "Function" of R&D Input

This section sets out to answer question (b).

It should be stressed immediately that we are referring here to output quantitatively and not qualitatively. The purpose of R&D is to generate knowledge. By changing the R&D input, we are concerned at this stage only with the change in the *quantity* of knowledge resulting—we are not interested in the *quality* of the knowledge, whether it is in the form of new products, new processes, new techniques, or whether it is commercially useful to the firm in question. Thus we are sidestepping for the time being the various other factors internal and external to the firm that determine the quality of the output.

This is bound to result in abstraction, but it is a necessary simplification when considering the main criticism of the "production function relating inputs to outputs" hypothesis—the assertion that, if the input is known, useful things can be said *ex ante* about the likely output. The criticism is that history bears witness to the high incidence of accidental discoveries, and that uncertainties are too great at the beginning of development programs to allow the assumption of an input-output relationship. If this criticism were valid, one would not be justified in using R&D as a surrogate for innovative output.

The "production function" hypothesis may be defended on three grounds. First, the mere fact that industries devote so much effort to innovation suggests that historical experience has not been entirely negative—that money is spent on R&D in the expectation of a worthwhile output. Second, in identifying the "target" for an R&D program (e.g., a new type of amplifier), there are almost always several possible routes to that target. If a certain line of inquiry does prove unrewarding (e.g., carbon fiber blades in the RB211 jet engine), an alternative solution can be explored (titanium alloy blades). Unpredictable obstacles can usually be overcome, although there may be heavy costs attached to the alternative solution. Third, to quote Freeman (1970), "The logical fallacy lies in assuming that, because accidental features are present in *indi-*

vidual cases, it is therefore impossible to make useful statistical generalizations about a *class* of phenomena."

This last defense is not completely watertight. Taking the scientific-instrument industry, there may well be sufficient numbers of products being developed concurrently to allow the assumption of a statistical relationship between R&D inputs and innovative outputs. However, the same does not apply to the aircraft industry, where only a handful of civilian products are being developed at any one time. Only if we took the world aircraft industry would we (possibly) find a statistically sufficient sample. Thus, if this last argument were our only defense, one would not be justified in comparing R&D inputs to the aircraft industries in countries A and B, and anticipating (quantitative) outputs related to these inputs. Fortunately, we are partially covered in this case by the second argument.

Qualitative Aspects of Innovation

Qualitative aspects have to be considered in relation to both inputs and outputs. It should be borne in mind that we are mainly interested in assessing whether the assertion of consistent relationships between innovative inputs and outputs holds water in comparing R&D-intensities across countries.

With regard to inputs, we first have to make assumptions about the balance of R&D between basic research, applied research and experimental development (as distinguished in the standard Frascati definitions). The respective contributions of these activities to innovation have always been a matter of controversy, and again it would appear that their relevance varies from industry to industry. In the chemical and drug industries, the emphasis is on basic and applied research; in mechanical engineering, it is on experimental development. We shall assume that, within each industry group, countries divide their resources equally. Second, it has to be assumed that R&D teams are equally skilled and equally well managed in each country. Little research has been done to suggest that this is or is not the case. Third, we have to assume that equivalent industries in each country benefit equally from sources of knowledge external to the firm—that the OECD countries in question have equal access to knowledge and to innovation-enhancing new products. This would certainly be unrealistic if we were considering countries with industrial infrastructures at widely different levels of development. It would nevertheless appear reasonable to assume that, restricting ourselves to the ten major OECD economies, external sources of knowledge have a marginal (and roughly equal) influence on innovative output in comparison with in-house R&D.

With regard to outputs, we have already touched on the qualitative differences in physical outputs that may arise from industries having different specializations.[4] The output of the innovation process has also to be considered from the point of view of its commercial quality. It was pointed out earlier that various tasks besides R&D (marketing, tooling, etc.) have to be carried out before a new product can be launched on the market. The "commercial quality" of the innovation will depend on the efficiency with which these tasks are performed.

R&D expenditures give no indication of the resources devoted to these activities. It is thus possible that a firm will spend large sums on R&D relative to its competitors, but that its innovative performance will be relatively poor. This emphasizes the point that R&D inputs cannot be used as a surrogate for the *quality* (technical, commercial, or otherwise) of the innovative output. They are a necessary but not sufficient condition for the successful exploitation of new knowledge in international marketplaces.

A related point needs stressing. Technological innovation is usually defined as "the technical, industrial and commercial steps which lead to the maketing of new and improved manufactured products and to the commercial use of new and improved production processes and equipment." Regarded as a capital investment in the Johnsonian sense, resources devoted to the innovation process do not include the capital needed to achieve commercial penetration in world markets. Just as R&D expenditures do not necessarily lead to good innovative performance, so good innovative performance does not necessarily lead to increased shares of world markets; productive efficiency and resource constraints, and the low receptiveness of domestic markets, can all limit the necessary productive expansion.

R&D STATISTICS

R&D statistics were first collected, on a national basis, by the U.S. and U.K. governments in the 1950s. Internationally comparable statistics, based on agreed definitions and industrial classifications, were first assembled by the OECD, the year of the first comprehensive survey being 1963/1964 (some countries reporting figures for 1963, others for 1964).[5] Statistics have subsequently been published by the OECD for the years 1967, 1969 and 1971.

We are concerned here with R&D inputs to the Business Enterprise Sector.[6] The OECD uses a 20-industry classification of manufacturing industry, chosen so that the industries represented are approximately technologically distinct. The compatibility of this classification with the ISIC and SITC classifications is shown in Table A.1.

Table A.1

Assumed Correspondence between ISIC, SITC and OECD R&D Industry Classifications

OECD		ISIC	SITC
5.	Electricals	383	72, 891.1
6.	Chemicals	351, 352 - 3522	231, 266, 5 - 541
7.	Drugs	3522	541
10.	Aircraft	3845	734 + 711.4
11.	Motor vehicles	3843	732
12.	Ships	3841	735
15.	Ferrous metals	371	67
16.	Nonferrous metals	372	68
17.	Fabricated metal products	381	69, 812, 894
19.	Instruments	385	861, 862
20.	Mechanical machinery	382	71 - 711.4
22.	Food, drink, tobacco	311 to 314	01, 022 to 024, 032, 046 to 048, 053, 055, 061, 062, 09, 111, 112, 122, 211
23.	Textiles, leather clothing	321 to 324	61, 65, 841, 851
24.	Rubber, plastics	355, 356	62, 893
26.	Stone, clay, glass	361, 362, 369	66 - 667
27.	Paper, printing	341, 342	64, 892
28.	Wood, furniture	331, 332	243, 63, 82
29.	Total		

Data are presented in the OECD manuals on both R&D expenditures and manpower. Only expenditures will be considered here. R&D manpower statistics are in general unreliable, and are not available on a comparable basis for all the countries under consideration.

Product-Field vs. Industry-Group Classification

There are two distinct ways of classifying industrial activities: by Product Field and by Industry Group. As their names imply, the Product Field classification distinguishes R&D (or exports or employment, etc.) according to the technological characteristics of the product in question; the Industry Group classification distinguishes according to the principal activities of the parent industry.

The Product Field classification is capable of greatest precision and disaggregation, and is almost always preferable. But it is not always practical. It is applied mainly in the collection of Trade Statistics (SITC), as detailed information can be recorded when commodities pass through customs. The Industry Group classification is more widely used, especially in national accounting. For instance, it is used to classify industrial activities in the UK Census.

In submitting R&D data to the OECD, member-countries are requested, for practical reasons, to break it down by industry group—the reporting unit being the firm (enterprise) classified according to main industrial activity. However, when production in a firm is known to be highly diversified, countries are also requested to use the establishment as the main reporting unit.

As is admitted by the OECD, the majority of R&D data is reported according to enterprise, diversification or no diversification. This is especially unsatisfactory given the trend toward greater and greater diversification (and vertical integration) that has been evident in recent years.[7]

The exercise of correlating R&D and trade statistics can be criticized on the grounds that one is correlating on the basis of different classifications (industry group and product field)—at least for the majority of OECD countries. The type of error that can result may be illustrated with reference to the German textile industry. OECD statistics demonstrate that it increased its share of World Trade between 1962 and 1972 (mainly due to its superiority in synthetic fibers—a research-intensive technology), but it performed little R&D relative to other countries. The most likely explanation is that synthetic fibers were classified in the R&D statistics under "chemicals" (production of synthetic fibres in Germany being concentrated in the chemical industry).[8]

However, this difficulty should not be exaggerated. The results of a study carried out in the United Kingdom provide some comfort. The United Kingdom and France are alone among OECD countries in collecting their R&D statistics according to a product-field classification.[9] Their statistics are therefore not strictly comparable with those of other OECD member countries. However, the recent Department of Industry study suggested that, for the United Kingdom, the discrepancies arising from the different data-collection systems were, in general, sufficiently small to be counted as insignificant.[10]

Discrepancies may be rather more significant for countries where the technique of collecting R&D statistics has been less successfully mastered than in the United Kingdom. On the whole, we can be reasonably confident when comparing the statistics of five of our selected countries (United States, United Kingdom, Sweden, Japan, Canada). The EEC-6 statistics will have to be treated with much greater caution.

Differences in Coverage of R&D Surveys from Country to Country

The 1963-1964 R&D survey was, for most countries, the first that they had carried out. As a result, the number of firms to which questionnaires were sent, the proportion of questionnaires returned, and the quality of the replies, was in general rather low. For Germany, in particular, the 1963-1964 (and to a lesser extent the 1967 and 1969) R&D statistics are unrepresentative partly because a private organization (Stifterverband für die Deutsche Wissenschaft), with less persuasive power than government in matters of data-collection, conducted the surveys.

Apart from Germany, all countries estimated that in 1967, 1969, and 1971 surveys, over 85 percent of formal R&D had been identified. Some countries "grossed up" their data to approximate 100 percent coverage. It should also be remembered that all countries face the same problems of being unable to measure innovative work conducted outside formal R&D laboratories, especially in small firms.

Problems of Dissaggregation

Table A.2 demonstrates one of the most intractable problems we face in using the available statistics: the difficulty some countries have had in disaggregating their R&D returns. It is partly due to industrial diversification and highly concentrated industrial structures, partly due to secrecy laws that allow firms to withhold information. The Dutch statistics show the problem at its most acute.

In the statistical tests we wish to carry out, the size of the sample is important. If, for instance, we wished to rank R&D-intensities in the car industry, avoiding estimation where disaggregation has not been possible, our sample would contain five countries: France, Belgium, Germany, the UK and Japan (see Table A.2). Not only is this sample statistically insufficient, it omits countries contributing a substantial proportion of total trade (e.g., Sweden).

There are three courses open to us: leave the statistics as they are, and wherever statistics are aggregated, leave them out of our sample (as for the car industry above); estimate wherever aggregation has taken place (e.g., apportion $1,000 million of the $1,324 million spent in the United States on chemicals and drugs to chemicals, $324 million to drugs); or take a more aggregated classification, grouping industries wherever difficulties have occurred in disaggregation (e.g. chemicals with drugs). Grouping industries together makes some sense when R&D cost structures and intensities are approximately equivalent. Thus to group chemicals with drugs is to an extent justifiable; to group aircraft with motor vehicles and ships is unjustifiable.

We have followed the second of the above courses. Wherever possible, secondary sources have been used to check these estimates; otherwise we have had to rely on our own judgment. It is hoped that the margin for error has been kept to a tolerable level.

Three industrial categories have been omitted in Table A.3: petroleum refining (the dominance of multinational companies raises doubts about both R&D and trade statistics), other transport equipment, and other manufactured goods (the industries in these categories being too diffuse). In addition, "rubber and plastics" have been included in "chemicals." Some countries have been unable to extract plastics R&D from general chemical R&D.

Table A.2

R&D Expenditures (Company-funded): 1967

National Currencies

Country Industry-Group**	U.S m$	Belgium mFB	France mFF	Germany mDM	Italy 10^9 Lire	Netherlands mFL	U.K. £m	Sweden mKr	Japan 10^9 Yen	Canada mC$
5	1409	1013	503	1124	25.0	(with 20)	97.1	267	83.7	72.4
6	1324	1797	525	1449	29.0		41.2	34.0	72.0	33.8
7		310	195		16.3	373	28.8	68.4	17.9	7.9
8*	385	80.0	151	35.8	0.9		9.5	7.7	2.7	20.7
10	756	17.9	162	29.9			23.2	(with 13)	–	20.8
11		37.5	464	635	47.7		43.7	(with 13)	37.4	
12	976	7.3	11.9	0.9			1.3	10.0	4.3	3.0
13*		6.3	n.a.	14.2			1.8	53.1	1.4	
15	135	297	71.2	336	4.9	497	13.4	120	19.7	5.8
16	85	207	62.6	56.1			5.5		10.6	18.4
17	148	168	(with 15)	29.8	0.3		6.7	15.6	6.0	3.9
19	301	94.0	235	87.6	3.2		10.7	11.8	7.2	2.6
20	958	256	230	456	4.1		50.5	178	29.4	12.3
22	165	107	40.5	19.3	0.9	60.0	18.4	30.1	12.9	8.2
23	53	121	120.4	23.4	2.4	23.6	12.6	7.4	9.5	3.4
24	157	18.7	49.7	46.6	8.5	7.5	5.1	7.5	4.6	2.8
26	125	291	118.1	32.1	0.5	6.9	9.7	25.4	9.0	2.9
27	85	57.1	22.6	13.4	0.6	8.8	8.3	36.3	5.0	20.8
28	64	20.2		2.0	1.5	6.7		5.0	0.5	1.2
29*		17.6	46.5	5.0			3.4	2.3	9.5	2.6
30	7126	4924	3008	4397	146	984	391	880	343	243

Source: OECD (1970).
*Industry-group 8, 13 and 29 denote petroleum products, other transport equipment and other manufactures, respectively.
**Industry-group classification as per Table A.1.

Table A.3

R&D Expenditures (Company-funded): 1967
Disaggregated according to own estimates

National Currencies

Country Industry-group**	U.S. m$	Belgium mFB	France mFF	Germany mDM	Italy 10^9 Lire	Netherlands mFl	U.K. £m	Sweden mKr	Japan 10^9 Yen	Canada mc$
5	1409	1013	702	1124	25.0	215*	97.1	267	83.7	72.4
6	967*	1797	525	1086	29.0	206*	41.2	34.0	72.0	33.8
7	357*	310	195	362*	16.3	69.0*	28.8	68.4	17.9	7.9
24	157	18.7	49.7	46.6	8.5	7.5*	5.1	7.5	4.6	2.8
10	756	17.9	162.	29.9	19.0*	45.3*	23.2	3.1*	–	20.8
11	869*	37.5	464	635	22.2*	39.4*	43.7	50.0*	37.4	2.5*
12	71*	7.3	11.9	0.9	3.2*	14.7*	1.3	10.0	4.3	0.5*
15	135	297	35.2	336	3.5*	19.4*	13.4	86.5*	19.7	5.8
16	85	207	62.6	56.1	1.5*	10.5*	5.5	33.4*	10.6	18.4
17	148	168	36.1*	29.8	0.3	13.5*	6.7	15.6	6.0	3.9
19	301	94.0	36.1	87.6	3.2	38.2*	10.7	11.8	7.2	2.6
20	958	256	230	456	4.1	88.2*	50.4	178	29.4	12.3
22	165	107	50.5*	19.3	0.9	60.0	18.4	30.1	12.9	8.2
23	53	121	130	23.4	2.4	23.6	12.6	7.4	9.4	3.4
26	125	291	118	32.1	0.5	6.9	9.7	25.4	9.0	2.9
27	85	57.1	15.6*	13.4	0.6*	8.8*	6.5*	36.3	5.0	20.8
28	22*	20.2	7.0*	2.0	0.2*	6.7*	1.8*	5.0	0.5	1.2
30	6741	4820	2831	4340	140	873	376	869	330	220

* Figures estimated ** Industry-group classification as per Table A.1 *Source:* OECD (1970)

Source of Funds

The OECD surveys indicate whether R&D in the Business Enterprise Sector is company-funded, government-funded, funded by other national enterprises, or funded from abroad. As few countries were able to break down funds from the latter two sources according to their product groups, they were excluded. While one would especially like to include funds from abroad, they constituted less than 8 percent of company-funded R&D expenditures in all countries, so that there is some justification in leaving them out.

Without exception, all the identified statistical tests of the Leontief paradox and other trading phenomena have considered *total* (civilian and military) expenditure only. This makes little sense, as the great majority of military R&D in the countries under consideration is internalized, and has a debatable impact on international trading patterns. Furthermore, much of the arms traffic is linked to foreign aid programs, especially in the United States.

Ideally, we should like to sum company funding with commercially oriented government funding in industry (e.g., United Kingdom Launching Aid).[11] This we could only do by carrying out detailed investigations in each of our selected countries. Ideally, we should also allow for spin-off effects from military R&D;[12] and for know-how transferred free of charge from government laboratories and universities.

Here we shall concentrate on company-funded R&D, without correction for spin-offs from other R&D activities. We shall, however, compare the strengths of correlations using company-funded and government-funded R&D statistics in those industries where government funding has historically been a significant proportion of the total.

R&D-Intensities

There are two main reasons why it is preferable to compare R&D-intensities across countries rather than comparing absolute levels of R&D expenditure. First, by relating R&D expenditures to outputs (here value-added), an indication is given of the intensiveness with which an industry develops new technologies, as discussed previously. R&D-intensity can act as a proxy for technological dynamism. High absolute levels of R&D expenditure may be an expression of little more than industry size. Second, the use of R&D-intensities partially averts the problems arising from exchange rates and price inflation. OECD manuals report R&D expenditures in national currencies. These may be translated into, say, dollars, by applying appropriate currency exchange rates. However, this is not enough. To quote the Frascati manual: "The official exchange rate is based on external trade and money markets and does not necessarily reflect the domestic price level of countries or the real cost of R&D activity." Thus one needs to calculate "research exchange rates" related specifically to current and capital costs of R&D from country to country.

Research exchange rates were estimated by Freeman and Young (1965) for Belgium, France, Germany, Netherlands, and the United Kingdom—all in relation to U.S. costs. They have also been estimated for Japan.[13] These exchange rates have not been updated, although it is generally agreed that R&D costs have converged substantially (OECD, 1975b). Table A.4 compares very approximately absolute R&D expenditures (in relation to their likely output), using Freeman and Young's exchange rates and applying a GNP deflator (for want of a better one) to take account of inflation.[14]

R&D-intensities relate R&D expenditures to some measure of an industry's productive output, e.g., sales, value added, employees. Best of these measures for our purposes is value added. As R&D-intensity is a ratio, and as both R&D expenditures and value added are subject to approximately equivalent rates of inflation, the exchange rate problem is largely diverted. The assumption is, however, being made that factor intensities of R&D and value added are equivalent for the industries under scrutiny. If they significantly diverged, differing factor costs would still unbalance our comparisons across countries (e.g., the research effort in Japanese chemicals would be underestimated).

Value-added statistics have been taken from the United Nations "Growth of World Industry" publication.[15] These statistics have two main problems: the different treatment of taxation from country to country; and, as for the R&D statistics, the difficulties some countries have had in disaggregating.

As far as taxation is concerned, there is little that we can do without going to a great deal of trouble; the UN source gives little or no indication of cross-country discrepancies. Thus we have to accept the statistics

Table A.4

R&D Expenditures (Company-funded): 1967

@ 1962 currency exchange rates; Freeman & Young RER applied;
1963 constant prices

m$

Country Industry-Group*	U.S.	Belgium	France	Germany	Italy	Netherlands	U.K.	Sweden	Japan	Canada
5	1272	29.2	191	429	71.5	90.4	377	64.4	587	76.0
6,7,24	1337	61.4	209	571	153	118	292	26.5	664	46.7
10	582	0.5	44	11.4	25.7	19.0	90	0.8	–	21.8
11	784	1.1	126	243	85.8	16.6	170	12.0	262	2.7
12	64	0.2	3.2	0.3	15.2	6.2	5.1	2.4	30.2	0.6
15,16,17	332	19.4	36.4	161	14.9	23.7	100	32.8	255	29.4
19.20	1136	10.1	72	208	20.9	52.9	238	45.8	257	15.7
22	149	3.1	13.9	7.4	2.6	25.2	71.5	7.3	90.5	8.6
23	48	3.5	35.3	8.9	3.4	9.9	49.2	1.8	66.6	3.6
26	113	8.4	32.1	12.3	1.4	2.9	37.7	6.1	63.1	3.1
27,28	97	2.2	6.3	5.9	2.3	6.4	32.4	10.0	38.6	23.1
30	6046	136.4	770	1664	412	372	1472	210	2321	231

* Industry-group classification as per Table A.1
Source: OECD (1967)

at face value, but admit that different taxation systems are possible sources of error.

The UN "Growth of World Industry" also contains gross output statistics. These are, in general, more complete than the value-added data. Where industrial sectors have been aggregated in the value-added tables (e.g., drugs with industrial chemicals), the breakdown between these sectors has been estimated from gross output figures. Thus, if gross output in the chemical industry is given as twice that in the drug industry, value added is assumed to be in the same proportion. Naturally, there is an implicit assumption here that the factor intensities of the two industries are identical; fortunately, industries tend to be grouped in such a way that factor intensities approximate.

The Consistency of R&D Surveys

Ideally, it would be useful to build a time lag into our correlations, to take account of the period between midpoint of R&D expenditure and the exploitation of new products and processes in international trade. The time lag might vary from around three to ten years, depending on the industry in question. It has already been pointed out that the coverage of the 1963-1964 survey left much to be desired. Unfortunately, some countries' returns for the later years 1967, 1969, and 1971 are inconsistent. For instance, Swedish expenditures on transport equipment increased by 20 percent between 1967 and 1969, by 134 percent between 1969 and 1971; Belgian company-funded R&D expenditures are not available for the year 1969 (they have been estimated from total expenditures, following patterns for 1967 and 1971); and French statistics are generally inconsistent, partly due to the switches between product- and industry-group classifications noted earlier. In a few cases where inconsistency was blatant between years (e.g., French expenditures on instruments), and the reason is self-evident, expenditures have been redistributed between categories (e.g., from instruments to electricals in the French case).

Errors arising from inconsistency between survey years have been kept to a minimum by aggregating R&D expenditures and value added for the years 1967, 1969, 1971, the ratio of the two measures giving average R&D-intensities, as set out in Table A.5. This gives an inadequate time lag, but it is the best that we can do in the circumstances.

Table A.5

Averaged R&D-Intensities, 1967, 1969, 1971

Percentages

Country Industry-Group*		U.S.	Belgium	France	Germany	Italy	Nether-lands	U.K	Sweden	Japan	Canada
5	(a)	7.09	6.60	7.05	7.85	5.05	8.28	7.35	9.33	6.48	5.14
	(b)	15.68	7.13	13.39	9.03	6.98	9.16	11.85	10.75	6.63	7.34
6,24	(a)	3.69	7.52	4.20	5.33	2.46	7.22	3.17	6.40	4.26	2.09
7	(a)	8.41	14.74	10.27	9.14	10.06	13.46	10.00	25.13	6.79	3.68
	(b)	9.37	16.76	10.93	9.35	11.45	13.80	10.64	25.40	6.79	4.82
10	(b)	45.54	2.52	55.78	–	7.93	13.21	35.50	–	–	14.82
11	(a)	6.02	0.19	4.41	4.89	5.01	9.40	4.54	4.07	4.06	0.30
12	(a)	3.78	0.24	0.50	0.16	2.74	2.52	0.62	1.54	1.78	0.35
15	(a)	0.95	1.14	0.75	1.12	0.30	2.61	1.21	2.01	1.86	0.66
16	(a)	2.08	3.27	2.20	2.28	0.81	8.49	1.93	1.17	3.04	2.83
17	(a)	0.85	1.71	0.40	0.24	0.15	1.48	0.72	2.68	0.52	0.27
19	(a)	5.27	6.04	1.44	4.29	1.68	11.89	3.55	4.63	4.16	1.51
	(b)	7.53	9.08	3.25	6.47	1.91	13.13	4.54	4.69	4.23	3.69
20	(a)	3.96	1.86	1.01	1.98	0.45	5.11	2.25	3.76	1.89	1.18
	(b)	5.02	1.92	1.69	2.56	0.66	5.65	2.77	3.92	2.08	1.51
22	(a)	0.61	0.32	0.22	0.08	0.13	1.89	0.93	0.55	1.03	0.29
23	(a)	0.24	0.40	0.52	0.08	0.36	0.57	0.92	0.57	0.65	0.20
26	(a)	1.60	1.24	1.21	0.37	0.06	0.55	1.00	1.51	1.19	0.33
27,28	(a)	0.43	0.31	0.10	0.08	0.08	0.32	0.40	0.55	0.43	0.46
30	(a)	3.01	1.95	1.73	2.51	1.66	4.06	2.36	2.54	2.57	1.14

(a): Company-funded
(b): Total, all sources

*Industry-group classification as per Table A.1
Source: OECD (1970, 1972, 1975a).

NOTES

1. This is an overstatement, as innovations sometimes originate outside formal R&D departments. We are assuming that these innovations form a minor part of the total, in the historical period being discussed.

2. The costs of innovation are discussed at greater length by Pavitt and Walker (1976). It should be stressed that Mansfield's and Stead's results were based on relatively small samples of innovations. The percentages quoted here do not necessarily represent R&D costs for the industries taken as a whole.

3. As in other areas of economic analysis, it is useful to normalize inputs by some measure of productive output, thereby indicating the relative intensiveness with which the industry uses the inputs in question. In this case, relative R&D-intensity (R&D as a percentage of value added) acts as a proxy for technological "dynamism," although it should be stressed that this applies strictly to industries in which new technologies are in the main internally generated. In more traditional "recipient" industries, R&D-intensity should ideally be supplemented by a productivity indicator (e.g., value-added per employee) if an indicator of technological progressiveness is required.

4. There is a further assumption here that equivalent industries assign equal priority to product and process innovation. It seems reasonable.

5. Only OECD member countries have been included in the surveys.

6. Data are also available for the general government, private nonprofit, and higher education sectors.

7. To illustrate the problem activities related to manufacturing a digital voltmeter could, according to the industry group classification, be correctly classified under "textiles," if the principal activity of the parent company happens to fall under that heading.

8. The unexpectedly low R&D-intensity reported for the German shipbuilding industry might be similarly explained.

9. The French used a product-field classification for 1963, 1969, and 1971; industry-group classification for 1967.

10. "Resources devoted to R&D by manufacturing industry," *Economic Trends*, March 1974.

11. Even if we could subtract military funding from the total, problems would remain—e.g., the large amounts spent by governments on "civilian" space R&D.

12. Unfortunately, these are indeterminate. Boretsky (1969) suggests that 10 percent of military R&D should be added to company-funded R&D, but admits that it is a completely arbitrary figure.

13. After applying currency exchange rates, Freeman and Young estimated R&D costs (for a given "output") for 1964 to be: United States 100, Belgium 59, Germany 59, Netherlands 53, France 67, United Kingdom 56. Japanese costs were by the same reckoning approximately 25.

14. Despite the approximations used in deriving Table B.4, it is interesting in its illustration of the scale of funding in the selected countries. It is especially notable that Japanese R&D effort was already very substantial by 1967.

15. Value-added statistics are collected according to the main activities of industry groups.

Appendix B

The Measurement of Trading Performance

In Chapter IV, we shall be exploring the hypothesis that "innovativeness" is a significant constituent of comparative advantage, as revealed by appropriate measures of trading performance, in certain industries. In particular, we wish to take into account *changes* in trading patterns, exploring their links with innovative effort.

If attention is restricted to the trading performance of a single country, "exports as a percentage of sales" and "excess of exports over imports, as a percentage of sales" are perhaps the least imperfect measures. Gruber, Mehta and Vernon (1967) made use of them to show that the performance of U.S. innovation-intensive industries in international markets was superior to that of the more traditional industries, with clear implications for the location of comparative advantage in the U.S. economy. The main deficiency of these measures for our purpose is that they fail to express a country's export performance *relative* to that of its competitors.

The problem we face in comparing changes in trading performance is how to "rate" the performance of different countries, especially when the absolute size of their contributions to world trade are of a different order of magnitude. Somehow the relative concepts of "good" and "bad" performance have to be encompassed by the selected measure. As demonstrated previously, it is possible, provided certain conditions hold, to rank countries according to the extent of their innovative efforts. Unless we can similarly rank trading performance, our attempt to demonstrate empirically relationships between innovative effort and export performance will be abortive.

Two contrasting measures suggest themselves. The first is derived by considering absolute changes in export values over a period of time, the second by considering ratios (or rates of growth) over the same period of time.

The first of these measures we shall call the "normalized ratio of export differences," R_D, differences here meaning changes in dollar value. It may be expressed as follows:

$$(R_D)_{t_1 \rightarrow t_2} = \frac{\text{Country i's difference in exports of product-group j}}{\text{Ten-country difference in exports of product-group j}}$$

$$\div \frac{\text{Country i's difference in exports of total manufactured goods}}{\text{Ten-country difference in exports of total manufactured goods}}$$

If χ_{ij} = the exports of country i in product-group j at time t_1, and $\chi_{ij} + \Delta\chi_{ij}$ = similar exports at time t_2, then R_D may be rewritten as:

$$(R_D)_{t_1 \rightarrow t_2} \equiv \frac{\Delta\chi_{ij}}{\sum_{i=1}^{10} \Delta\chi_{ij}} \div \frac{\sum_{j=1}^{15} \Delta\chi_{ij}}{\sum_{i=1}^{10} \sum_{j=1}^{15} \Delta\chi_{ij}}$$

$$= \frac{\Delta\chi_{ij}}{\sum_{j} \Delta\chi_{ij}} \div \frac{\sum_{i} \Delta\chi_{ij}}{\sum_{i} \sum_{j} \Delta\chi_{ij}}$$

It can be seen that this measure gives the contribution of country i to the absolute increase in the value of exports occurring over the time period in product-group j, *relative* to country i's contribution to the increase in the value of total exports of manufactured goods. Thus, if $R_D >$ 1, the increase in exports in product-group j is proportionally greater than that for exports as a whole. These normalized ratios of export differences are set out in Table B.1 (values of exports in 1963-1965 and 1971-1973 are shown for reference in Tables B.2 and B.3.).

The criticisms that may be leveled at this measure all arise from one failing—it disregards the initial level (χ_{ij}) of a country's exports in a particular commodity. Thus, if the exports of an infant industry (e.g., the

Table B.1

Normalized Ratios of Export Differences (1971 - 1973/1963 – 1965)
(R_D)

Country Industry-Group*	U.S.	Belgium	France	Germany	Italy	Netherlands	U.K.	Sweden	Japan	Canada
5	1.139	0.579	0.796	1.020	0.911	0.964	0.856	1.033	1.568	0.397
6,24	1.018	1.293	1.186	0.960	0.737	1.980	1.181	0.324	0.797	0.397
7	0.868	1.040	1.150	1.242	1.247	1.273	2.211	0.628	0.229	0.237
10	–	–	–	–	–	–	–	–	–	–
11	0.994	0.894	0.966	0.989	0.670	0.165	0.564	0.879	1.108	2.704
12	0.167	0.180	0.537	0.706	0.396	1.190	0.472	1.738	3.609	0.218
15	0.243	2.237	1.054	1.037	0.714	0.841	0.491	1.179	1.858	0.336
16	0.561	2.286	0.739	0.830	0.327	0.883	2.099	0.948	0.345	2.722
17	0.769	0.929	0.964	1.077	1.419	1.000	1.110	1.196	1.080	0.521
19	1.524	0.191	0.666	1.091	0.494	1.432	1.491	0.592	1.413	–
20	1.308	0.409	0.881	1.355	1.103	0.510	1.248	1.080	0.719	0.621
22	0.544	1.602	2.143	0.553	0.807	3.836	1.411	0.372	0.180	0.264
23	0.309	1.530	1.251	1.003	2.673	1.267	0.748	0.499	0.869	0.225
26	0.449	1.580	1.330	1.051	2.510	0.746	1.045	0.581	0.639	0.412
27,28	0.888	1.197	0.758	0.768	0.839	0.895	0.666	3.372	0.243	3.219
30	1.000	1.000	1.000	1.000	1.000	1.000	1.000	1.000	1.000	1.000

*Industry-group classification as per Table A.1

Swedish drug industry) increase at a significantly greater rate than the exports of its established competitors, R_D will underrate the infant industry's relative performance. Since no account is taken of χ_{ij}, the relatively low absolute increase will read as an indication of relatively poor performance. The opposite is the case for an established industry starting with a large share of the market (e.g., Canada and wood products). Its share of the world market may actually decline, but the incremental value of its exports will still be substantial in relation to the incremental value of its total exports; R_D will overrate its performance in relation to other countries.

A bias is therefore induced in favor of the industry starting with a large share of world markets, against the industry with a small share (relative to both its competitors and the national average). In the first case,

$$\frac{\Delta\chi_{ij}}{\sum_{j=1}^{15}\Delta\chi_{ij}} >> \frac{\sum_{i=1}^{10}\Delta\chi_{ij}}{\sum_{i=1}^{10}\sum_{j=1}^{15}\Delta\chi_{ij}},$$

artificially uprating R_D; in the second case, the inequality is reversed, artificially depressing R_D.

The second measure we shall call the "normalized ratio of export shares," R_S. The first step in deriving this measure is to calculate ratios of export shares, r_S. As r_s in itself can be regarded as a proxy for relative performance, it is useful to discuss its merits in relation to R_D first.

$$(r_S)_{t_1 \to t_2} = \frac{\text{Country i's exports in product-group j } (t_2)}{\text{Country i's exports in product-group j } (t_1)} \div \frac{\text{Ten-country exports in product-group j } (t_2)}{\text{Ten-country exports in product-group j } (t_1)},$$

$$= \frac{\text{Country i's export share in product-group j } (t_2)}{\text{Country i's export share in product-group j } (t_1)}$$

r_s thus compares rates of growth of, rather than absolute differences between, a country's exports in relation to a ten-country average. Using the same definitions for χ_{ij} and $\Delta\chi_{ij}$ as before, r_s may be rewritten as:

Table B.2

Exports 1963 - 1965

Million U.S. $

Country Industry-Group*	U.S.	Belgium	France	Germany	Italy	Netherlands	U.K.	Sweden	Japan	Canada	TOTAL
5	4764	680	1376	3961	1035	1662	2700	609	1928	432	19147
6	6561	984	2848	5430	1539	1661	3149	369	1413	964	24918
7	816	75.3	360	579	158	185	504	38.1	85.8	36.8	2838
10	3556	388	470	241	288	506	931	13.0	16.9	626	7036
11	5086	954	2053	6525	1345	209	4484	616	938	531	22741
12	213	68.3	328	687	158	356	298	769	1578	31.3	4486
15	1826	3066	2411	3798	778	672	1838	851	2902	595	18937
16	1479	1284	550	940	200	289	1206	196	224	2375	8743
17	1830	554	840	2235	680	246	1482	483	1271	205	9876
19	1216	38.8	250	1166	162	122	519	61.6	538	212	4286
20	13454	988	2705	10752	2640	955	6960	1717	1440	1275	42886
22	3197	601	2524	661	806	2414	1845	205	611	1085	13949
23	2194	2156	3140	2642	3610	1580	3380	279	4092	226	23299
24	504	92.7	367	378	189	113	406	80.8	274	36.3	2441
26	712	608	511	946	359	174	621	77.0	543	50.7	4602
27	1689	318	589	705	230	448	799	1104	240	2500	8622
28	630	224	375	458	212	158	154	842	386	1622	5061
30	49727	13080	21897	42204	14389	11750	31276	8261	18481	12803	223868

Source: OECD, Trade by Commodities, Series B.
*Industry-group classification as per Table A.1.

Table B.3

Exports 1971 - 1973

Million U.S. $

Country Industry-Group*	U.S.	Belgium	France	Germany	Italy	Nether-lands	U.K.	Sweden	Japan	Canada	TOTAL
5	12167	2440	5035	13806	4186	4430	5591	2289	12360	1625	12360
6	13233	4817	7606	14190	3677	7385	6942	1066	6324	2110	67350
7	1495	456	997	2022	678	625	1404	161	270	123	8231
10	12183	288	1295	600	471	614	2895	123	108	1337	19914
11	14977	5118	8849	21131	4897	933	7403	2805	12206	12947	91266
12	506	215	994	2524	527	1277	728	1531	8049	207	16558
15	2918	7765	5756	10706	2486	2340	2985	2176	11440	1291	49863
16	2355	2954	1367	2865	472	898	2911	566	776	4337	19501
17	3798	1667	2586	6328	2614	1377	2960	1248	4101	820	27509
19	3079	149	826	3147	484	896	1468	243	2307	114	12713
20	28389	3177	9823	33734	9351	3528	14376	4805	9842	4548	121573
22	4779	2780	6931	3047	2055	7338	3978	476	1148	1439	33971
23	3690	5629	7434	9862	10512	4293	5269	884	8409	732	56714
24	744	368	1312	1296	720	330	790	214	909	135	6818
26	1210	1428	1555	2678	1842	539	1224	238	1269	262	12245
27	3403	1209	1699	2821	896	1395	1697	2510	837	4336	20803
28	1789	1146	999	2031	994	492	379	2167	594	4598	15189
30	110715	41606	65075	132788	46862	38690	63000	23502	80949	40961	644147

Source: OECD, Trade by Commodities, Series B
*Industry-group classification as per Table A.1.

$$(r_S)_{t_1 \to t_2} \equiv \frac{\chi_{ij} + \Delta\chi_{ij}}{\chi_{ij}} \div \frac{\sum_{i=1}^{10} (\chi_{ij} + \Delta\chi_{ij})}{\sum_{i=1}^{10} \chi_{ij}}$$

$$= \left(1 + \frac{\Delta\chi_{ij}}{\chi_{ij}}\right) \div \left(1 + \frac{\sum_i \Delta\chi_{ij}}{\sum_i \chi_{ij}}\right)$$

An immediate advantage of r_S is apparent: it is mathematically more stable than R_D. The presence of the integer on either side of the fraction (resulting from χ_{ij} being represented in both numerators) has a "damping" effect—averting some of the instability inherent in the ratio of differences.

r_S is preferable to R_D in that it incorporates the base value χ_{ij}, but unfortunately it also induces a bias into the calculations, in the opposite direction from that observed for R_D: it overrates the performance of the infant industry, underestimates the performance of the established industry. Just as R_D took inadequate account of relative *rates* of increase of exports, so r_S (and R_S) takes inadequate account of the relative *scale* of the increase. Giving an extreme case to illustrate the point, if an infant industry increases its share of world trade from 1 percent to 3 percent, its export share will have tripled; an industry with a large share of the market (say 35 percent) is bound, however it has performed, to have a lower value of r_S, as its export share cannot triple. But algebraically, if $\Delta\chi_{ij} >> \chi_{ij}$, and

$$\frac{\Delta\chi_{ij}}{\chi_{ij}} >> \frac{\sum_{i=1}^{10} \Sigma\chi_{ij}}{\sum_{i=1}^{10} \chi_{ij}}$$

the performance of the industry in question will be overrated; if the inequality is reversed, it will be underrated.

It could be argued, however, that provided the extreme cases are omitted (e.g., wherever a country's share of trade in a commodity is initially <2 percent or >25 percent), the bias associated with r_s is more in accord with present-day economic conditions than that associated with R_D, in that gaining entry to world markets is made difficult in some industries by the dominance of the multinational companies, and by oligopolistic market structures. It may therefore be preferable to err in the direction of exaggerating the performance of the small rather than the large industry.

Ratios of export shares are listed in Table B.4. It is apparent that some countries (e.g., Belgium, Japan, and the Netherlands) increased their export shares in nearly all areas of manufacture, while other countries suffered corresponding decreases (e.g., the United States and the United Kingdom). To claim that differences in innovative activity alone could account for these rises and falls in economic fortune would be to overstate the case, even in the high technology industries. As we know only too well in Britain, economic growth can be hindered by balance of payments difficulties, shortages of skilled labor, low investment, labor immobility and a host of other socio-economic circumstances acting singly or in combination. There is therefore some point in normalizing the ratio of export shares by a measure of a country's trading performance taken as a whole, so that an industry's performance is assessed relative to that of its international competitors *and* to that of its parent economy. The resulting normalized ratio of export shares is as follows:

$$(R_S)_{t_1 \rightarrow t_2} = r_S \div \frac{\text{country i's share of total manufactured exports } (t_2)}{\text{country i's share of total manufactured exports } (t_1)}$$

Values for R_S are set out in Table B.5. What to they signify? If $R_S > 1$, an industry's share of exports has either grown at a faster rate than, or has decreased at a lesser rate than, the parent country's share of total manufactured exports. Thus R_S for both German and United Kingdom mechanical machinery industries is greater than unity, despite their relatively increasing and decreasing shares of world trade. Put another way, Germany and the United Kingdom have, relative to competing countries, increasingly specialized in the export of mechanical machinery.

Unfortunately, R_S only compensates for different rates of growth; it does not allow for differences in scale. Which measure should we then resort to in ranking export performance, so that we can carry out our

Table B.4

$$\frac{\text{Export Shares 1971 - 1973}}{\text{Export Shares 1963 - 1965}} \; (r_s)$$

Country Industry-Group*	U.S.	Belgium	France	Germany	Italy	Nether-lands	(EEC-6)	U.K.	Sweden	Japan	Canada
5	0.765	1.076	1.096	1.044	1.211	0.798	(1.028)	0.621	1.126	1.920	1.124
6	0.746	1.810	0.983	0.967	0.883	1.643	(1.118)	0.816	1.068	1.656	0.809
7	0.632	2.091	0.955	1.204	1.479	1.164	(1.214)	0.961	1.463	1.086	1.146
24	0.528	1.421	1.280	1.227	1.364	1.045	(1.265)	0.697	0.949	1.188	1.329
10	1.211	0.263	0.973	0.880	0.579	0.428	(0.610)	1.099	3.444	2.250	0.754
11	0.734	1.336	1.074	0.807	0.909	1.109	(0.920)	0.411	1.133	3.245	6.090
12	0.642	0.855	0.821	0.995	0.903	0.971	(0.939)	0.663	0.540	1.382	1.812
15	0.607	0.962	0.837	1.070	1.214	1.321	(1.010)	0.617	0.971	1.497	0.825
16	0.714	1.031	1.114	1.367	1.057	1.390	(1.175)	1.083	1.295	1.555	0.819
17	0.745	1.080	1.106	0.973	1.381	2.012	(1.124)	0.717	1.037	1.159	1.433
19	0.854	1.300	1.115	0.910	1.008	2.474	(1.067)	0.954	1.326	1.446	0.182
20	0.744	1.135	1.280	1.107	1.248	1.300	(1.165)	0.728	0.988	2.411	1.259
22	0.614	1.898	1.128	1.892	1.047	1.248	(1.298)	0.885	0.952	0.772	0.544
23	0.691	1.072	0.973	1.534	1.196	1.119	(1.181)	0.640	1.300	0.844	1.330
26	0.639	0.883	1.144	1.064	1.928	1.164	(1.163)	0.740	1.162	0.878	1.928
27	0.835	1.574	1.196	1.658	1.614	1.290	(1.441)	0.880	0.943	1.446	0.719
28	0.946	1.702	0.888	1.477	1.561	1.038	(1.322)	0.819	0.858	0.512	0.944
30	0.744	1.106	1.033	1.093	1.131	1.143	(1.093)	0.700	0.989	1.524	1.112

*Industry-group classification as per Table A.1

Table B.5

Normalized Ratios of Export Shares $\frac{(1971 - 1973)}{(1963 - 1965)}$ (R_s)

Country Industry-Group*	U.S.	Belgium	France	FRG	Italy	Netherlands	U.K.	Sweden	Japan	Canada
5	0.988	0.973	1.061	0.955	1.071	0.698	0.887	1.139	1.260	1.011
6,24	0.943	1.604	0.990	0.903	0.829	1.404	1.146	1.067	1.037	0.745
7	0.817	1.891	0.924	1.102	1.308	1.018	1.373	1.479	0.713	1.031
10	1.565	0.238	0.942	(0.805)	0.512	0.374	1.570	(3.482)	(1.476)	0.678
11	0.948	1.208	1.040	0.738	0.804	0.970	0.587	1.146	2.129	5.477
12	0.829	0.773	0.795	0.910	0.798	0.850	0.947	0.546	0.907	1.629
15	0.784	0.870	0.810	0.979	1.073	1.156	0.881	0.982	0.982	0.742
16	0.922	0.932	1.078	1.251	0.934	1.216	1.547	1.309	1.020	0.737
17	0.963	0.976	1.071	0.890	1.221	1.760	1.024	1.049	0.760	1.289
19	1.103	1.175	1.079	0.833	0.891	2.164	1.363	1.341	0.949	0.164
20	0.961	1.026	1.239	1.013	1.103	1.137	1.040	0.999	1.582	1.132
22	0.793	1.716	1.092	1.731	0.926	1.092	1.264	0.963	0.507	0.489
23	0.893	0.969	0.942	1.403	1.057	0.979	0.914	1.314	0.554	1.196
26	0.826	0.798	1.107	0.973	1.705	1.018	1.057	1.175	0.576	1.734
27,28	1.099	1.494	1.030	1.451	1.437	1.035	1.184	0.924	0.570	0.741
30	1.000	1.000	1.000	1.000	1.000	1.000	1.000	1.000	1.000	1.000

*Industry-group classification as per Table A.1.

correlations with R&D intensities? Can some composite measure be constructed that combines the best features of both R_S and R_D? Perhaps the best that can be done is simply to add the values of R_S and R_D in Tables B.1 and B.5. We are justified in doing this as both R_S abd R_D are subject to errors induced, in opposite directions, by the same variable (industry size); to an extent, errors are canceled by summation. It should be stressed, however, that $R_S + R_D$ is not an ideal measure; the degrees of error induced by comparing ratios and differences are not strictly symmetrical. As indicated above, R_S is more stable than R_D, so that R_D can be expected to have slightly more "weight" in the composite than R_S.

REFERENCES

Baldwin, R. E., "Determinants of the Commodity Structure of U.S. Trade," *American Economic Review* 61, 1971, pp. 126–146.

Beckerman, W., "The British Economy in 1975," National Institute of Economic and Social Research, Cambridge University Press, 1965.

Bhagwati, J. B., "The Pure Theory of International Trade. A Survey," American Economic Association, *Surveys of Economic Theory,* Vol. II, 1968, pp. 156–239.

Boretsky, M., "Trends in U.S. Trade and the International Competitiveness of U.S. Industry," mimeo, 1969.

Caves, R. E., and R. W. Jones, "World Trade and Payments: An Introduction," Boston: Little, Brown, 1973.

Chesney, F., and C. M. Cooper, "International Economic Exchanges," OECD *Gaps in Technology,* Paris, 1970.

Cooper, C., and R. Kaplinsky, "Second-hand Equipment in a Developing Country: A Study of Jute-Processing in Kenya," ILO, Geneva, 1974.

Drèze, J., "Quelques réflexions sereines sur l'adaptation de l'industrie belge au Marché Commun," *Comptes rendus des Travaux de la Société Royale d'Economique Politique de Belgique,* No. 275, December 1960.

Falk, C., Dynamics and Forecastings of R&D Funding, *Technological Forecasting and Social Change,* July 1974.

Freeman, C., et al., "Chemical Process Plant: Innovation and the World Market," *National Institute Economic Review,* No. 45, August 1968.

———, "The Plastics Industry: A Comparative Study of Research and Innovation," *National Institute Economic Review,* No. 26, November 1963.

———, "Research and Development in Electronic Capital Goods," *National Institute Economic Review,* November 1965.

———, "Measurement of Output of Research and Experimental Development," UNESCO, 1970.

———, and A. Young, "The Research and Development Effort in Western Europe, North America and the Soviet Union; An Experimental International Comparison of Research Expenditures and Manpower in 1962," OECD, Paris, 1965.

Gruber, W. H., D. Mehta, and R. Vernon, "The R&D Factor in International Trade and International Investment of United States Industries," *Journal of Political Economy,* 75, 1967, pp. 20–34.

———, and R. Vernon, "The Technology Factor in a World Trade Matrix," in *The Technology Factor in International Trade,* National Bureau of Economic Research, New York, 1970, pp. 233–273.

Hansson, K-E, "A General Theory of the System of Multilateral Trade," *American Economic Review* 42, 1952, pp. 58–68.

Harcourt, G. C., "Some Cambridge Controversies in the Theory of Capital," New York: Cambridge University Press, 1972.

Harman, A. J., "The International Computer Company: Innovation and Comparative Advantage," Cambridge, Mass.: Harvard University Press, 1971.

Hirsch, S., "The United States Electronics Industry in International Trade," *National Institute Economic Review,* November 1965.

———, "Capital or Technology? Confronting the Neo-Factor Proportions and Neo-Technology Accounts of International Trade," *Journal of Kiel Institute of World Economics,* 1974.

Horst, T., "The Industrial Composition of United States Exports and Subsidiary Sales to the Canadian Market," *American Economic Review* 62, March 1972, pp. 37–45.

Hufbauer, G. C., "Synthetic Materials and the Theory of International Trade," London: Duckworth, 1966.

———, "The Impact of National Characteristics and Technology on the Commodity Composition of Trade in Manufactured Goods," in *The Technology Factor in International Trade,* New York: National Bureau of Economic Research, 1970, pp. 145–231.

Johnson, H. G., "Comparative Cost and Commercial Policy Theory for a Developing World Economy," Wicksell lectures for 1968.

Kaldor, N., "Causes of the Slow Economic Growth of the United Kingdom," New York: Cambridge University Press, 1966.

Lamfalussy, A., "Investment and Growth in Mature Economies," London: Macmillan, 1961.

Leontief, W. W., "Domestic Production and Foreign Trade: The American Capital Position Reexamined," *Proceedings of the American Philosophical Society,* 1953, pp. 332–349.

Linder, S. B., "An Essay on Trade and Transformation," Stockholm, Sweden: Almqvist and Wiksell, 1961.

Maizels, A., "Industrial Growth and World Trade," National Institute of Economic and Social Research, Cambridge University Press, 1971.

Mann, P. F. E., "Licensing Technology: The Process Licensor's Point of View," *Chemistry and Industry,* 1968, pp. 1374–1379.

Mansfield, E., *et al.,* "Research and Innovation in the Modern Corporation," New York: Macmillan, 1971.

Meade, J. E., "A Geometry of International Trade," London: Allen & Unwin, 1952.

Minhas, B., "The Homohypallagic Production Function," *Journal of Political Economy,* April 1952.

OECD, Directorate of Scientific Affairs, A Study of Resources devoted to R&D in OECD Member countries in 1963/64, Vol. 2, Statistical Tables and notes, Paris, 1968.

———, Directorate of Scientific Affairs, International Survey of the Resources devoted to R&D in 1967 by OECD Member countries, Vol. 1, The Business Enterprise Sector, DAS/SPR/70.7, Paris, 1970.

———, Directorate of Scientific Affairs, International Survey of the Resources devoted to R&D in 1969 by OECD Member countries, Vol. 1, The Business Enterprise Sector, DAS/SPR/72.25, Paris, 1972.

———, "Science Policy in the USSR," Paris, 1969.

———, Directorate of Scientific Affairs, Survey of the Resources devoted to R&D in 1971 by OECD Member countries, Vol. 1, The Business Enterprise Sector, DSTI/SPR/75.5, Paris, 1975a.

———, Trade by Commodities, Series B, Paris, 1963–1965, 1971–1973.

———, Trends in the Level and Pattern of R&D Expenditures in the OECD Area since 1971, SPT/MIN(75)5, Paris, 1975b.

Pavitt, K., and W. B. Walker, "Government Policies Towards Industrial Innovation: A Review," *Research Policy,* Vol. 5, No. 1, 1976.

Posner, M. V., "International Trade and Technical Change," *Oxford Economic Papers,* Vol. 13, No. 3, October 1961.

Reuben, B., and M. Burstall, "The Chemical Economy: A Guide to the Technology and Economics of the Chemical Industry," London: Longmans, Green, 1973.

Rothwell, R., "Innovation in Textile Machinery: Some Significant Factors in Success and Failure," Science Policy Research Unit Occasional Paper No. 2, June 1976a.

———, "Picanol Weefautomaten: A Case Study of a Successful Textile Machinery Builder," *Textile Institute and Industry,* March 1976b.

Saunders, C., "From Free Trade to Integration in Western Europe?," London: Chatham House, 1975.

Sawers, D., and R. Miller, "The Technical Development of Modern Aviation," London: Routledge & Kegan Paul, 1968.

Schott, B., and W. Müller, "Process Innovations and Improvements as a Determinant of the Competitive Position in the International Plastic Market," *Research Policy,* Vol. 4, No. 1, 1975.

Schumpeter, J. A., "Capitalism, Socialism and Democracy," New York: Harper & Brothers, 1942.

Sciberras, E., "Multinational Electronics Companies and National Economic Policies," Greenwich, Conn.: JAI Press, 1976.

Shepherd, G., "International Trade in Cotton-type Textiles: A Case-Study of Comparative Advantage," Unpublished Ph.D. thesis, 1974.

Stead, H., "The Costs of Technological Innovation," *Research Policy,* Vol. 5, No. 1, 1976.

Stobaugh, R. B., "The Product Life Cycle, U.S. Exports and International Investment," unpublished Ph.D. thesis, Harvard University, 1968.

Surrey, A. J., and J. H. Chesshire, "The World Market for Electric Power Equipment: Rationalization and Technical Change," Science Policy Research Unit, University of Sussex, 1972.

Townsend, J., "Innovation in Coal Mining Machinery," Science Policy Research Unit occasional paper No. 3, December, 1976

United Nations, The Growth of World Industry, 1972 edition: Vol. 1, General Industrial Statistics 1962–1971, New York, 1974.

Vernon, R., "International Investment and International Trade in the Product Cycle," *Quarterly Journal of Economics,* May 1966, pp. 190–207.

———, "The Location of Economic Activity," in *Economic Analysis and the Multinational Enterprise,* J. H. Dunning, ed., London: Allen and Unwin, 1974.

Wells, L. T. (ed.), "The Product Life Cycle and International Trade," Cambridge, Mass.: Harvard University Press, 1972.

Woytinsky, W. S., and E. S. Woytinsky, "World Commerce and Governments," New York: Twentieth Century Fund, 1955.

Index

Automation. (*See* Production)

Balance of payments, 1, 110
Baldwin, R. E., 12
Beckerman, W., 79
Bhagwati, J. B., 11
Boretsky, M., 18, 101
Burstall, M., 39

Capital, 5, 11. (*See also* Investment)
  accumulation, 9, 36
  abundance, 14, 33
  cheap, 30, 71
  costs, 12, 72, 77, 97
  deepening, 78
  definition, 7–8, 17
  endowments, 2, 9, 32, 64
  equipment, 3, 7, 17
  expenditure, 78
  intensive, 2, 6, 7, 8, 12, 16–17, 25, 33, 37, 39, 40, 78, 80
  investment, 24, 89
  markets, 17
  mobility, 3, 7, 10, 11, 18, 22, 28, 29, 39
  resources, 32
  social, 7
  transfer, 17
  venture, 77
  widening, 78
Cartels, 32
Caves, R. E., 4, 11
Cheshire, J. H., 38
Chesney, F., 44
Classification:
  ISIC, 90
  industry group, 91, 99, 101
  product field, 91, 92, 99, 101
  SITC, 47, 48, 49, 50, 51, 52, 53, 90, 91
Comparative advantage, 1, 2, 7, 8, 9, 13, 14, 16, 17, 23, 24, 30, 31, 32, 33, 35, 36, 40, 54, 59, 60, 63, 64, 70, 79, 103
Competition, 6, 11, 12, 13, 14, 16, 20, 22, 23, 24, 25, 28, 29, 30, 31, 32, 33, 35, 36, 38, 40, 43, 60, 61, 64, 65, 70, 71, 72, 76, 78, 79, 85, 89, 103, 106, 110
  imperfect, 5
  perfect, 3, 7
Consumer preferences, 3, 4, 6, 8, 12
Cooper C., 37, 44

Drèze, J., 8
Dumping:
  anti-, 32

Economic growth, 36, 65, 78
Employment patterns, 53
Exchange rates, 1, 43, 97, 98, 101

Factor-intensity reversals, 6
"Factor-price equalization" theorem, 2–3
Falk, C., 79
"Footloose," definition, 23
Freeman, C., 17, 30, 38, 83, 87, 97, 98, 101

Government:
  funding, 69, 96
  intervention, 8, 25, 69, 79
  investment grants, 17
  laboratories, 23, 96
  spending, 101
  subsidies, 79
Gruber, W. H. 35, 63, 70, 103

Hansson, K-E., 11
Harcourt, G. C., 11
Harman, A. J., 38
Heckscher-Ohlin theory, 2, 3, 4, 5, 6, 8, 9, 11, 12, 17, 61
Hirsch, S., 14, 17, 19, 25, 36, 63
Horst, T., 79
Hufbauer, G. C., 10, 17, 18, 63

Imitation, 13, 14, 16, 18, 19, 22, 23, 30, 38, 77
Income levels, 8, 9, 14, 54
Innovation 13, 14, 15, 16, 17, 18, 19, 20, 22, 23, 24, 25, 28, 29, 30, 31, 32, 34, 35, 36, 37, 38, 39, 41, 48, 54, 62, 63, 64, 65, 66, 69, 71, 72, 73, 75, 76, 77, 78, 80, 81, 83, 84, 85, 86, 87, 88, 89, 92, 101, 103, 110
Investment, 16, 23, 24, 29, 30, 31, 32, 33, 36, 37, 39, 64, 65, 70, 71, 73, 77, 78, 89, 110. (*See also* Capital)

Johnson, H. G., 12, 17, 25, 35, 89
Jones, R. W., 4, 11

Kaldor, N., 79

Labor. (*See also* Manpower)
  cheap, 17, 71, 75
  costs, 2, 3, 12, 14, 20, 32, 33, 72, 75, 76, 77
  definition, 7
  endowment, 2, 9, 64
  intensive, 2, 3, 5, 6, 7, 16–17, 20, 33, 34, 40
  mobility, 3, 7, 11, 110
  productivity, 2, 5, 20, 24, 25, 65
  saving devices, 14, 20, 23, 36, 37, 77, 78, 80
  scarcity, 14, 20
  skills, 5, 7, 12, 17, 20, 23, 24, 25, 32, 34, 110
  wages, 32
Laissez-faire, 3
Lamfalussy, A., 78
Leontief, W. W., 6, 11, 12
  paradox, 5, 7, 16, 17, 96
Licensing, 22, 28, 30, 31, 38, 70, 71, 75
Linder, S. B., 8, 9, 10, 12, 14

Mann, P. F. E., 40
Manpower, 84. (*See* Labor)
  qualified, 18
  R & D statistics, 91
  skilled, 23, 25
Mansfield, E., 84, 85, 101
Marketing, 22, 24, 29, 89
Marshall, A., 11
Mehta, D., 35, 63, 70, 103
Mill, J. S., 11
Miller, R., 38
Minhas, B., 12

Monopoly, 1, 8, 9, 13, 16, 18, 19, 22, 30, 31, 39, 54, 64, 72, 76, 86
Müller, W., 40
Multinational companies, 39, 53, 70, 71, 75, 93, 110

Natural Resources, 1, 6, 7, 23
Neoclassical theories of international trade, 1–8, 9, 10, 11, 34, 35, 64, 79, 80
  assumptions, 3, 5, 13
  simplifications, 4
  tests, 4–8
  validity, 17

Obsolescence, 32, 33
Oligopoly, 25, 28, 32, 36, 76, 110

Patents, 19, 22, 30, 39, 83, 84
Pavitt, K., 101
Posner, M. V., 13
Price, 4, 31, 39
  advantage, 2
  commodities, 2, 3
  competition, 32, 65, 78
  elasticity, 16, 25, 30, 32, 33, 60
  inflation, 97
  intensive, 24
  relative, 2, 3, 11, 25, 44
  wars, 32
Processes, 20, 31, 35, 38, 40, 64, 67, 77, 78, 81, 85, 87, 99
  production, 16, 19, 23, 29, 30, 32, 39, 72, 89
  technology, 29, 30, 31, 65
Procurement, preferential, 76
Product behavior, 19, 25, 35
Product concentration, 47
Product cycle, 7, 10, 13, 14, 15, 16, 17, 18, 19, 20, 22, 23, 25, 29, 30, 32, 34, 35, 36, 38, 39, 40, 80, 83
Product development, 13, 14, 19, 20, 22, 23, 25, 28, 34, 35, 38, 85
Product differentiation, 8, 9, 16, 33, 54, 61, 73
Product quality, 73
Product specialization, 51, 53, 54, 59
Product stability, 14, 19, 24, 25, 29, 33, 34, 38, 39
Production, 1, 6, 7, 9, 11, 23, 35, 41, 43, 53, 54, 61, 70, 71, 72, 77, 78, 79, 81, 86, 91, 97, 101
  automation, 33
  batch, 20
  costs, 2, 13, 16, 17, 22, 25, 28, 29, 30, 31, 32, 33, 37, 38
  development, 18, 21, 22, 29, 65, 72
  efficiency, 32, 89
  factor intensities, 3, 4, 34
  function, 87
  learning, 14, 22
  location, 14, 16, 22, 31, 32, 34, 39, 75, 76
  mass, 16
  modern practices, 73
  processes, 39, 89
  relocation, 16, 17, 24, 34, 64, 80
  scale of, 3, 8
  stability, 29, 32, 34
  transfer, 18, 19, 28, 30, 32, 33, 73, 75
Productivity, 20, 21, 24, 25, 32, 65, 78, 81, 101
  labor 2, 5, 65
Profitability, 16, 39

Research & development (R & D), 22, 29, 35, 54, 59, 60, 61, 62, 63, 64, 66, 67, 68, 69, 70, 71, 74, 75, 78, 86, 87, 88, 90, 92, 93, 100, 101, 102, 113
  expenditure 7, 18, 61, 67, 72, 73, 76, 77, 79, 84, 85, 89, 91, 94, 95, 96, 97, 98, 99
  Frascati definition, 76, 84, 88
  surveys, 76, 90, 92, 96, 99
Research exchange rates, 97
Resource endowments, 6
Reuben, B., 39

Ricardo, 1, 2, 4, 6, 11
Risk, 25, 78
Rothwell, R., 24, 37, 38
Rybczynski theorem, 3

Saunders, C., 53
Sawers, D., 38
Scale economies, 8, 10, 13, 14, 16, 18, 22, 30, 31, 38, 40
Schott, B., 40
Schumpeter, J. A., 34, 72, 81
Sciberras, E., 39
Servicing, 25
Shepherd, G., 37
Spearman rank correlation coefficients, 59, 60, 68, 75
Spin-off, 96
Standardization, 8, 16, 17, 19, 24, 25, 28, 29, 30, 32, 33, 38, 40, 80
Statistical tests, 66, 67, 77, 81, 93, 96
Stead, H., 84, 85, 101
Strategic goods, 8
Stobaugh, R. B., 19, 31, 39, 40
Surrey, A. J., 38

Tariff barriers, 1, 5, 8, 11, 16, 18, 30, 34, 39, 60, 70
Taxation, 97, 99
Technical change, 7, 20, 24, 25, 28, 33, 35, 36, 49, 65, 77, 80
Technical leadership, 22, 36
Technology:
  access to, 3
  high, 7
  import of, 71, 75
  stability, 7, 14, 34, 80
  static, 2–3, 13
  transfer, 28
Technology gap theory, 7, 13–14, 17–18, 19, 39
Townsend, J., 28
Trade 9, 13, 14, 40, 93, 99, 109
  bilateral, 2, 4, 5, 11, 43
  flows, 18, 50
  free, 1, 3
  geographical concentration, 43, 44, 47
  models, 1
  multilateral, 4, 43
  patterns, 6, 8, 10, 12, 36, 41–61, 69, 70, 80, 96, 103
  percent of G.D.P., 42
  performance, 36, 41, 63, 66, 67, 69, 70, 71, 72, 73, 74, 75, 76, 85, 103, 110
  shares, 36, 47, 48, 49, 54, 55–58, 64, 65, 66, 69, 71, 76, 110
  theories, 1, 2, 5, 7, 8, 10, 63, 81
Trademarks, 8
Transport costs, 8, 12, 16, 30

Value added, 66, 72, 96, 97, 99, 101, 102
Vernon R., 14, 16, 17, 18, 19, 24, 25, 35, 36, 37, 63, 70, 103

Walker, W. B., 101
Wells, L. T., 19
Woytinsky, W. S., 61

Young, A., 97, 98, 101